CONTEMPORARY PERSPECTIVES ON THE FREUDIAN DEATH DRIVE

Contemporary Perspectives on the Freudian Death Drive provides a sustained discussion of the death drive from the perspective of different psychoanalytic traditions. Ever since Freud introduced the notion of the death drive, it has been the subject of intense debate in psychoanalysis and beyond.

The death drive is arguably the most unsettling psychoanalytic concept. What this concept points to is more unsettling still. It uniquely illuminates the forces of destruction and dissolution at work in individuals as well as in society. This book first introduces Freud's use of the term, tracing the debates and developments his ideas have led to. The subsequent essays by leading Viennese psychoanalysts demonstrate the power of the death drive to illuminate psychoanalytic theory, clinical practice, and the study of culture. Since this book originally arose from a conference in Vienna, its final segment is dedicated to the forced exile of the early Viennese psychoanalysts due to the Nazi threat. Due to its wide scope and the many perspectives it offers, this book is a tribute to the disturbing relevance of the death drive today.

Contemporary Perspectives on the Freudian Death Drive is of special interest to psychoanalysts, psychotherapists, social and cultural scientists, as well as anyone intending to understand the sources and vicissitudes of human destructiveness.

Victor Blüml is a psychiatrist and psychoanalyst (Vienna Psychoanalytic Society/IPA). He is Assistant Professor at the Department of Psychoanalysis and Psychotherapy of the Medical University of Vienna, Austria. His main research interests include personality structure, psychotic phenomena, suicidality, and conceptual issues of psychoanalysis. He has published in numerous publications including psychiatric and psychoanalytic journals.

Liana Giorgi is a social and political scientist and psychoanalyst in private practice (Vienna Psychoanalytic Society/IPA). She is the author/editor of *Festivals and the Cultural Public Sphere* (Routledge 2011), *Democracy in the European Union* (Routledge 2006), and *The Post-Socialist Media: What Power the West?* (Avebury 1995). She is currently working on a book on the intellectual exchanges between psychoanalysis, social and political theory.

Daru Huppert is a psychoanalyst in private practice in Austria (Vienna Psychoanalytic Society/IPA); he has published numerous psychoanalytic articles on sleep, sexuality, disgust, and shame.

PSYCHOANALYTIC IDEAS AND APPLICATIONS SERIES

IPA Publications Committee

Gabriela Legorreta (Montreal), Chair and General Editor; Dominique Scarfone (Montreal); Catalina Bronstein (London); Larry Brown (Boston); Michele Ain (Montevideo); Samuel Arbiser (Buenos Aires); Udo Hock (Berlin); Rhoda Bawdekar (London), Ex-officio as IPA Publishing Manager; Paul Crake (London), Ex-officio as IPA Executive Director

Recent titles in the series include

CONTEMPORARY PERSPECTIVES ON THE FREUDIAN DEATH DRIVE

In Theory, Clinical Practice and Culture

Edited by
Victor Blüml, Liana Giorgi and Daru Huppert

Taylor & Francis Group

LONDON AND NEW YORK

First published 2019
by Routledge
2 Park Square, Milton Park, Abingdon, Oxon OX14 4RN

and by Routledge
52 Vanderbilt Avenue, New York, NY 10017

Routledge is an imprint of the Taylor & Francis Group, an informa business

British Library Cataloguing-in-Publication Data
A catalogue record for this book is available from the British Library

Library of Congress Cataloging-in-Publication Data
Names: Blüml, Victor, 1982– editor. | Giorgi, Liana, editor. | Huppert, Daru, 1973– editor.
Title: Contemporary perspectives on the Freudian death drive : in theory, clinical practice and culture / edited by Victor Blèuml, Liana Giorgi and Daru Huppert.
Description: Abingdon, Oxon ; New York, NY : Routledge, 2019. | Series: The international psychoanalytic ideas and applications series | Includes bibliographical references and index.
Identifiers: LCCN 2018051581 (print) | LCCN 2018053765 (ebook) | ISBN 9780429054044 (Master) | ISBN 9780429620492 (ePub3) | ISBN 9780429618345 (MobiPocket) | ISBN 9780429622649 (Pdf) | ISBN 9780367149338 (hardback : alk. paper) | ISBN 9780367149345 (pbk. : alk. paper)
Subjects: LCSH: Death instinct. | Freud, Sigmund, 1856–1939.
Classification: LCC BF175.5.D4 (ebook) | LCC BF175.5.D4 C66 2019 (print) | DDC 150.19/52—dc23
LC record available at https://lccn.loc.gov/2018051581

ISBN: 978-0-367-14933-8 (hbk)
ISBN: 978-0-367-14934-5 (pbk)
ISBN: 978-0-429-05404-4 (ebk)

Typeset in Palatino
by Apex CoVantage, LLC

CONTENTS

SERIES EDITOR'S FOREWORD

The Publications Committee of the International Psychoanalytic Association continues the series Psychoanalytic Ideas and Applications with the present volume, *Contemporary Perspectives on the Freudian Death Drive: In Theory, Clinical Practice and Culture*.

The aim of this series is to focus on the work of significant authors who have made outstanding contributions to the development of the psychoanalytic field. In so doing, the series will bring forward relevant ideas and themes, generated during the history of psychoanalysis, that deserve to be known and discussed by present-day psychoanalysts.

The relationship between psychoanalytic ideas and their applications needs to be put forward from the perspective of theory, clinical practice, and research in order to maintain their validity for contemporary psychoanalysis. The Publications Committee's objective is to share these ideas with the psychoanalytic community and with professionals in other related disciplines, so as to expand their knowledge and generate a productive interchange between the text and the reader.

The present volume, *Contemporary Perspectives on the Freudian Death Drive: In Theory, Clinical Practice and Culture*, contributes to the Publications Committee's goal of bringing forward and discussing in depth one of the most important and controversial concepts in psychoanalysis:

the death drive. Perhaps as a consequence of current sociocultural phenomena, such as the effects of climate change, terrorism, and massive immigration, this concept has received renewed attention in the last years. With this in mind, the present work is a timely re-evaluation of the death drive and, with it, the question of the destructive potential of human nature.

Starting with Freud's foundational ideas on the death drive, which created the "turning point" in his theory of the mind, the authors then trace the subsequent developments of the concept in psychoanalytic theory, proposing threads that can be observed in contemporary debates on the death drive. The editors' review of these debates raises questions concerning the definition of the concept, its conceptual status, or even the existence of the death drive. The ongoing attention to this topic shows that the concept has the potential to create much dialogue and debate in psychoanalysis. As the authors state: "The notion of the death drive seems to be very alive."

Skillfully organized in four parts, this volume first addresses theoretical aspects of the death drive from three different perspectives (British, French, and American). The second part focuses on manifestations of the death drive in clinical work, while a third part analyzes the mechanisms of the death drive in contemporary culture and society. A final part addresses the history of psychoanalysis in Austria and its connection with the notion of the death drive.

The authors' thorough overview of current psychoanalytic understanding from major psychoanalytic traditions on the topic of the death drive has resulted in this valuable book. They have succeeded in reawakening the need to reconsider the debate on the nature of human destructiveness. I am confident that it will be useful and of much interest not only to the psychoanalytic reader worldwide but to anyone interested in the complex and significant subject of the death drive. It will certainly be an important reference point for future debates and conceptual developments on the subject.

Gabriela Legorreta
Series Editor
Chair, IPA Publications Committee

CONTRIBUTORS

Thomas Aichhorn is a psychoanalyst in private practice, a member of the Vienna Psychoanalytic Society (VPS/IPA), and an archivist of the VPS. He lectures and writes on the theory and history of psychoanalysis, on Jean Laplanche's General Seduction Theory, on the psychoanalysis of adolescence, and on August Aichhorn's works and biography. He is editor of the correspondence of Anna Freud/August Aichhorn and of papers by August Aichhorn, Rosa Dworschak. and K.R. Eissler.

Victor Blüml, MD, MA, PhD, is a psychiatrist and psychoanalyst (Vienna Psychoanalytic Society/IPA). He is Assistant Professor at the Department of Psychoanalysis and Psychotherapy of the Medical University of Vienna, Austria. He studied medicine and philosophy in Vienna and Paris. His main research interests include personality structure, suicidality, psychotic phenomena, and conceptual issues of psychoanalysis. He has published in numerous publications including psychiatric and psychoanalytic journals.

Friedl Früh is a psychoanalyst (Vienna Psychoanalytic Society, IPA), training and supervising analyst of the VPS, and head of the training program in child analysis of the VPS. She has written numerous publications on Sigmund Freud's and Jean Laplanche's theories (e.g. "The Sexual Breast").

Liana Giorgi, PhD, is a psychoanalyst at the Vienna Psychoanalytic Society (VPS/IPA), a social and political scientist working in research and as a psychoanalyst in private practice. She is a graduate of MIT (USA) and the University of Cambridge (UK). She has published extensively in the fields of political sociology and European integration; some titles (as co-author and co-editor) are *Festivals and the Cultural Public Sphere* (Routledge 2011) and *Democracy in the European Union: Towards the Emergence of a Public Sphere* (Routledge 2006). She is currently working on a book on the intellectual exchanges between psychoanalysis, social, and political theory.

Daru Huppert, PhD, is a psychoanalyst (Vienna Psychoanalytic Society/ IPA) in private practice. He studied psychology in New York, Zurich, and Cambridge, and he also lectured on psychoanalysis at Cambridge University. He has published several articles on the topics of sexuality and sleep in psychoanalysis.

Tjark Kunstreich, MA, is a psychoanalyst (Vienna Psychoanalytic Society/IPA) and writer. He works in private practice and in the outpatient clinic of the VPS where he is head of the unit for severely traumatized patients. He is currently the managing director of the Vienna Psychoanalytic Academy, a joint outreach project of the two Vienna IPA-Societies. He has published on a variety of issues with a focus on trauma, destructiveness, psychosis, and history, and as well on homosexuality and its vicissitudes.

Fritz Lackinger, PhD, is associate professor for clinical psychology, psychotherapy, and psychoanalysis at the University of Klagenfurt, Austria. He is a member as well as training and control analyst of the Vienna Psychoanalytic Association (VPA) and the IPA. He is also a training therapist and training supervisor for Psychoanalytic Oriented Psychotherapy and for Transference Focused Psychotherapy, and president of the Vienna Psychoanalytic Association since 2015. Lackinger is editor of a book on psychodynamic psychotherapy with delinquents, and the author of many articles on clinical and theoretical questions of psychoanalysis.

Nadja Pakesch, MA, PhD in art history, is a psychoanalyst and member of the Vienna Psychoanalytic Society (VPS/IPA) and its working group on the history of psychoanalysis. She has further training in child and adolescence psychoanalysis, and has worked with minor unaccompanied refugees in the Integrationshaus Wien for many years. She also works in private practice.

Hemma Rössler-Schülein, MD, is a psychiatrist, psychoanalyst, RTP/IPA research fellow, supervising and training analyst of the Vienna Psychoanalytic Society (VPS), medical director of the outpatient clinic of the VPS (2009–2015), and since 2016 president of the VPS. Her publications in the field of psychotherapy research and conceptual questions in psychoanalysis include (with H. Löffler-Stastka) "Psychoanalysis and Psychoanalytic Oriented Psychotherapy: Differences and Similarities" in *Neuropsychiatrie* (2013), and "The Use of Phantasy in the Psychoanalytic Process" (2017).

August Ruhs, MD, is an associate professor, psychiatrist, and psychoanalyst (Vienna Psychoanalytical Association/IPA). From 2007 to 2015 he was president of the VPA, and until 2011 was deputy head of the Department of Psychoanalysis and Psychotherapy at the Medical University of Vienna. He is co-founder and president of the "Neue Wiener Gruppe/Lacan-Schule"; co-editor of the journal *texte. psychoanalyse. ästhetik. kulturkritik*; and has published in many publications in the fields of theoretical, clinical, and applied psychoanalysis.

Elisabeth Skale, MD, is a psychiatrist and psychoanalyst in private practice. She is training analyst at Vienna Psychoanalytic Society (VPS/IPA); Head of the Department of Theory/History/Culture of the Vienna Psychoanalytic Academy; and Austrian consultant of the European Psychoanalytic Film Festival (epff). Her publications are on theoretical and clinical psychoanalytic issues. She is co-editor (with B. Reith, et.al.) of *Initiating Psychoanalysis-Perspectives* (Routledge).

Jeanne Wolff Bernstein, PhD, is past president and supervising and personal analyst at the Psychoanalytic Institute of Northern California (PINC). She is on the faculty at PINC and at the Sigmund Freud Private University, Vienna, and the NYU postdoctoral program for psychoanalysis and psychotherapy. She was the 2008 Fulbright Freud Visiting

Scholar in Psychoanalysis at the Freud Museum, Vienna, Austria, and is the chair of the Scientific Advisory Board at the Freud Museum, Vienna. She is a member of the Vienna Psychoanalytic Association. She has published numerous articles on the interfaces between psychoanalysis, the visual arts, film, and Lacan.

Sylvia Zwettler-Otte, MA, PhD, is training analyst of the Vienna Psychoanalytic Society (VPS/IPA) and was president of the organization from 2000 to 2004, now member of the ethics committee. At the EPF Congress 2008 in Vienna she initiated the Forum on Psychoanalysis and Language. She has published several books in German and English, among them *Freud in the Media: The Reception of Psychoanalysis in Viennese Medical Journals 1895–1938* (2006), *The Melody of Separation – A Psychoanalytic Study of Separation Anxiety* (2011), and *The Sphinx and the Riddles of Passion, Love and Sexuality*, with contributions by Stefano Bolognini and Rainer Gross (Preface by Alain Gibeault) (2013).

ACKNOWLEDGEMENTS

This book initially developed from an international conference entitled "The Aim of all Life is Death – Debating the Death Drive Today" held in Vienna in July 2016. It was organized by candidates of the two Viennese psychoanalytic societies (Vienna Psychoanalytic Society and Vienna Psychoanalytic Association) in collaboration with the International Psychoanalytic Studies Organization (IPSO). We would first like to thank all those who were directly involved in the organization of the conference: René Diem, Esther Hutfless, Dago Kogoj, Tjark Kunstreich, Andrea Naderer, Barbara Pastner, Alberto Storari, and Roman Widholm. Our thanks also goes to IPSO, especially Nergis Güleç and Holger Himmighoffen, for their support, as well as to the Vienna Psychoanalytic Society and the Vienna Psychoanalytic Association, who supported the conference from the very beginning. We want to express our special gratitude to Viola Seibert, who was very helpful in all stages of the organization. The Sigmund Freud Museum, Vienna, generously offered us a lecture hall, in which the last part of the conference took place. We would like to thank the Publications Committee of the International Psychoanalytical Association for publishing our book under the aegis of the IPA, and Gabriela Legoretta, the chair of the Committee, for writing the foreword. Charles Bath of Routledge expertly guided the editing and publication process. It was a pleasure to work with him.

Last but not least, we want to express our gratitude to all the speakers at the conference for their contributions and for their willingness to substantially revise their work in order to make this publication possible.

The death drive: a brief genealogy of a controversial concept

Victor Blüml

Ever since Freud introduced the concept of the death drive[1] in "Beyond the Pleasure Principle" in 1920, it has been the subject of intense and impassioned debate among psychoanalysts. No other Freudian concept has been as controversially disputed as the idea of a fundamental force of destructiveness and dissolution. Many analysts regard it as ungrounded, as too speculative, or, simply, as too pessimistic. However, for many other analysts the death drive is an indispensable reference point for thinking about destructive and deadening phenomena encountered in the consulting room and beyond. In recent years there has even been a resurgence of interest in the topic of the death drive, which is indicated by an increasing number of relevant articles published in leading psychoanalytic journals (e.g. Bell, 2015; De Masi, 2015; Falcao, 2015; Penot, 2017). While the underlying reasons for this renewed attention to the notion of the death drive are manifold, it seems plausible that contemporary sociocultural developments contribute to it. The rise of populist movements on the far right with strong nationalist and xenophobic tendencies, recurrent terrorist attacks, and mass migration caused by civil war and political turmoil create an atmosphere of increasing anxiety and threat. Freud's "fateful question" as to whether cultural development could master the human drive of aggression and self-destruction seems more pressing than ever (Freud, 1930, p. 145): "The question of the existence of the death drive as part of the core of human psychology is, unfortunately, a practical and not merely a theoretical problem" (Kernberg, 2009, p. 1010).

In this light, the psychoanalytic exploration of the destructive potential of human nature seems of utmost importance with the notion of the death drive serving as a focal reference point for a deeper understanding of the psychological mechanisms involved.

Since the debates and discussions on the death drive have continued for almost a hundred years, any attempt to provide an overview of this concept necessarily will remain fragmentary and incomplete. Nevertheless, this introduction aims to sketch some of the main lines in the debate about this controversial term. As with so many of the basic psychoanalytic concepts, we first need to return to Freud's foundational ideas in order to gain a sense for the original meaning of the notion. Only then can we trace the subsequent developments, which often take up one or the other of the originally implied aspects, while deemphasizing or leaving out others.

Freud and the death drive

When Freud introduced the concept of the death drive in 1920 in "Beyond the Pleasure Principle", this was the starting point of his highly productive and innovative later works. This period notably included the introduction of the structural model of the psyche, a revised theory of anxiety and symptom formation, as well as, to return to our topic, the final dualistic drive theory, with opposing life and death drives. The motives that led Freud to completely reformulate his fundamental drive theory are complex and difficult to trace (cf. Laplanche, 1976; May, 2015). First, Freud felt the need to provide a metapsychological basis for a variety of clinical phenomena that could not readily be accounted for within the traditional model of the sexual and self-preservation drives. For example, repetition phenomena like recurring traumatic dreams and negative therapeutic reactions bear witness to a compulsion to repeat that lies beyond the workings of the pleasure principle, which hitherto had been thought to govern all psychic processes. Other salient phenomena include the merciless superego in melancholia, sadism, and masochism, as well as forms of destructiveness and hate that cannot be derived from the vicissitudes of the sexual drive alone. Several authors have high-lighted the role that the growing number of severely disturbed patients suffering from non-neurotic disorders in Freud's clinical experience played in his re-conceptualization of the drive theory (and, more gener-ally, in the new developments in his thought after the "turning point" of 1920) (Green, 2010). Another factor, of a more theoretical character, was Freud's basic tendency to think in dualistic terms, which had become threatened by the introduction of narcissism into psychoanalytic theory in 1914 (Laplanche, 2004). The discovery of the libidinal nature of large parts of the self-preservative drive led to a crisis in Freud's thinking; the danger of a monistic conception of the libido in a Jungian fashion now loomed large over the metapsychological project. Only via the introduc-tion of a new fundamental opposition between life and death drives could the dualistic balance be reinstated, which Freud deemed necessary to account for the pervasiveness of psychic conflict. Lastly, a growing scepticism or, more accurately, realism, regarding the powers and limi-tations of psychoanalytic treatment is thought to have been one of the decisive factors leading Freud to postulate an innate and fundamental force opposing psychic growth and improvement.

Turning to the characteristics of this new force, we find in the death drive the expression of the fundamental tendency of every living being to return to the inorganic state: *"the aim of all life is death"* (Freud, 1920, p. 38, emphasis as in original). The death drive aims at the reduction of all tension of life, at unbinding and dissolution. Freud saw the death drive as primarily directed towards the subject itself, its principal aim being self-destruction. The task of Eros, the great antagonist of the death drive, is to mitigate the auto-destructive potential of the death drive.

> The libido has the task of making the destroying instinct innocuous, and it fulfils the task by diverting that instinct to a great extent outwards – soon with the help of a special organic system, the muscular apparatus – towards objects in the external world. The instinct is then called the destructive instinct, the instinct for mastery, or the will to power.
>
> (Freud, 1924, p. 163)

To comprehend some of the controversies arising from the introduction of this drive, it is essential to note that the work of the death drive is not readily observable; it remains mute and by its very nature conceals its own activity. Only when it has been diverted outwards and fused with the life drives does it become discernible in the form of striking and loud phenomena, such as aggression and sadism. In the course of Freud's later writings a shift takes place; he increasingly pays more attention to the aggressive phenomena associated with the death drive instead of the more subtle and mute aspects originally addressed in "Beyond the Pleasure Principle." In this sense, he formulated in 1930: "This aggressive instinct is the derivative and the main representative of the death instinct which we have found alongside of Eros and which shares world-dominion with it" (Freud, 1930, p. 122). Nevertheless, he always conceptually differentiated between the death drive per se and aggression as one of its "derivatives" or "representatives." This distinction was to become repeatedly blurred by many later analysts who referred to the notion. Penot (2017) recently addressed this conceptual tension and argued that the Freudian death drive condenses two separate processes, which cannot be easily integrated under the umbrella of one concept alone, namely, the process of unbinding and dissolution on the one hand, and on the other hand open aggression and destructivity.

Adding to the complexity of Freud's idea was his insistence that the death drive never enters the stage alone, but only appears in the form of fusions with Eros:

> So far as the psycho-analytic field of ideas is concerned, we can only assume that a very extensive fusion and amalgamation, in varying proportions, of the two classes of instincts takes place, so that we never have to deal with pure life instincts or pure death instincts but only with mixtures of them in different amounts.
>
> (Freud, 1924, p. 164)

Besides the primarily mute nature of the death drive, its activity is so difficult to isolate and identify because of the ever-present element of Eros in even the most destructive phenomena. "Only by the concurrent or mutually opposing action of the two primal instincts – Eros and the death-instinct – never by one or the other alone, can we explain the rich multiplicity of the phenomena of life" (Freud, 1937, p. 243).

Initially, Freud introduced the notion of the death drive with considerable caution as a "speculation," which would need further scrutiny before it could be considered a basic psychoanalytic tenet. But, in the remaining 18 years of his life, he became increasingly convinced that this notion was indispensable and soon came to view the death drive as one of the foundational pillars of psychoanalytic theory: "To begin with it was only tentatively that I put forward the views I have developed here, but in the course of time they have gained such a hold upon me that I can no longer think in any other way" (Freud, 1930, p. 119). Freud's growing conviction was not shared by the majority of his colleagues and followers. On the contrary, the reaction of many analysts of the day ranged from outward rejection to silent disregard and negligence. The reasons for the controversial reception of the death drive concept were themselves manifold and heterogeneous. Freud believed that this refusal was not only motivated by scientific or rational considerations alone: "I presume that a strong affective factor is coming into effect in this rejection" (Freud, 1933a, p. 103). Much like Freud's early ideas about the centrality of sexuality had been met with considerable resistance by his contemporaries, his introduction of a fundamental self-destructive force at work in the individual aroused strong opposition, but this time also within the analytic circle itself. Martin Bergmann has argued "that Freud's death instinct theory had a traumatic impact on the psychoanalytic movement because it greatly limited the belief in the curative power of our therapeutic work" (Bergmann, 2011, p. 684). The assumption of a death drive also was a wounding blow for more optimistic views of human nature, which consider human destructivity primarily as a consequence of frustration. Therefore, analysts engaged in social revolutionary activities like Wilhelm Reich and Otto Fenichel rejected the idea of a fundamental death drive, instead highlighting the role of socioeconomic factors in the development of human destructivity. Many critics of the concept argued that Freud had introduced the notion primarily because of personal-biographical reasons. They cite Freud's deep grief at the loss of his favourite daughter Sophie and his good friend Anton von Freund at the time of his writing of "Beyond the Pleasure Principle" or the beginnings of his struggles with cancer as prime motivational forces rather than scientific reasoning (Ekstein, 1949; Jones, 1957).[2]

While the reactions just described seem to validate Freud's observation about the affective components involved in the acceptance or refusal of a theoretical argument, it does not exonerate us from a searching analysis of the issues at stake. We otherwise run the risk of theoretical self-immunization against any opposing claims. It is therefore necessary to gain a clearer idea about the conceptual and epistemological status of the notion of the death drive. Misunderstandings and misconceptions in this area seem to have been at the core of many objections and controversies regarding the death drive.[3] Perhaps unavoidably, Freud himself was not always clear about these issues, thereby paving the way for future misunderstandings. A central difficulty is related to the general character of Freudian metapsychology. Drive theory was one of the cornerstones of Freud's metapsychological conceptions; these conceptions do not refer to elements or forces that are directly observable in clinical practice but rather serve as a general and abstract frame of reference that organizes the observed material. Throughout his life, Freud was keenly aware of the dangers of ungrounded speculation, yet at the same time he considered a certain speculative element indispensable to provide a conceptual basis for the new science of psychoanalysis. This tension is reflected in the way in which metapsychology can be regarded: it can be considered as the foundation, upon which the entire system of psychoanalysis was to be constructed, as well as being seen as "a speculative superstructure of psycho-analysis, any portion of which can be abandoned or changed without loss or regret the moment its inadequacy has been proved" (Freud, 1925, pp. 32–33). This ambiguous nature of the metapsychological project is also expressed in Freud's famous remarks about the status of drives: "Instincts are mythical entities, magnificent in their indefiniteness. In our work we cannot for a moment disregard them, yet we are never sure that we are seeing them clearly" (Freud, 1933a, p. 95). For Freud, drives were part of the basic concepts and principles of psychoanalysis; due to their foundational nature they eluded further deduction or more precise definitions (cf. Freud, 1940, p. 159).

Consequently, the status of drive theory became the subject of fierce debates and intense criticism in many psychoanalytic schools (Schmidt-Hellerau, 2005). Given the high level of abstraction, a concept such as the death drive can never be directly inferred from experience, therefore complicating attempts at proving or refuting it. Empirical facts such as clinical observations or findings from neighbouring sciences can only ever provide indicators or indirect support for a theory like the death drive, never direct proof. Freud himself repeatedly fell into the trap of seeking to use such findings as direct evidence for the existence of the entity "death drive," most prominently by drawing on the biological discoveries of his day in "Beyond the Pleasure Principle." This line of reasoning could be considered to stand in the tradition of defining the truth of a concept as "correspondence with reality" and accordingly to make the presence or absence in empirical reality the sole criterion for the validity of a concept (cf. Hanly, 1990). Another approach would instead highlight the role of "internal coherence" within a certain theoretical system as the basic element of the truth of a concept (Armengou,

2009; Hanly, 1990). It is not the intention to advocate the abandonment of a truth-theory of correspondence for psychoanalysis – in fact, any scientific system needs to take into account both elements of truth – but it can reasonably be argued that it would constitute a methodological fallacy to discount a concept like the death drive purely on the grounds of one empirical finding or the other. In this sense, Schmidt-Hellerau convincingly states:

> That is why a question like "Is there such a thing as a *death drive*?" (which is usually answered with "no") represents a failure in thinking; the questions can only be "Are there phenomena that we can unite by a notion to be defined and called the *death drive*?" and "Does it make sense, or is it heuristically fruitful, to make use of such a concept?"
> (Schmidt-Hellerau, 2005, pp. 999–1000)

Trajectories of the reception of the death drive

The various psychoanalytic traditions gave different answers to these questions. As stated, the initial reception of the newly introduced concept was rather critical. As Jones put it with regards to Freud's "Beyond the Pleasure Principle":

> The book is further noteworthy in being the only one of Freud's which has received little acceptance on the part of his followers. Thus of the fifty or so papers they have since devoted to the topic one observes that in the first decade only half supported Freud's theory, in the second decade only a third, and in the last decade none at all.
> (Jones, 1957, p. 287)

Recently, Frank proposed a more nuanced view of the early reception of the death drive concept (2015). She traced Jones' statement back to an article by Brun (1953) and pointed to various inconsistencies in the appraisal of the magnitude of the initial rejection. Frank argued that as soon as Freud was able to provide clinical examples for the workings of the death drive (melancholia, guilt feelings) many analysts like Reik, Alexander, and Nunberg favourably took up the notion. She also highlighted the role that the forced emigration due to the rise of the Nazi regime of nearly all analysts who published on the death drive played for the subsequent history of the discourse on the death drive. In Germany (and Austria), the reception of the concept was impeded by

the prevailing effects of the terrors of Nazi rule and associated guilt feelings leading to defence mechanisms like denial at work in society and
within analytic associations. According to Frank, the rejection of the
death drive hypothesis in post-war Germany (and Austria) represents a
reaction formation against the traumatic experiences of the Nazi era. In
other parts of the world, the history of the discourse on the death drive
took different paths, but the impact of the forced emigration of the early
adopters and the dispersal of the Austrian and German analysts can be
observed in many areas and would warrant further research.

British and American perspectives

In Britain, for instance, the concept of the death drive played a sub-
stantial role in the controversial discussions that shook the British
Psychoanalytic Society in the 1940s following the arrival of the Viennese
analysts in London (King & Steiner, 1991). Melanie Klein was undoubt-
edly the most prominent early supporter of the idea of the death drive.
Already in her early psychoanalytic work with children and adolescents
in Berlin she had formed the idea of an "evil principle" accounting for
aggressive and destructive aspects of personality (Frank, 2015). Later
on, most likely influenced by the publication of "Civilization and Its
Discontents" in 1930, with its emphasis on aggression as the primary
derivative of the death drive, she incorporated the notion of the death
drive into her theoretical framework. In the process, Klein partly altered
the meanings and connotations of the term, without always making
these changes explicit, arguably in order to remain loyal to Freud and to
make her ideas more acceptable to the psychoanalytic community (De
Bianchedi et al., 1984). She was not very interested in metapsychological speculations or the biological underpinnings of the concept. Klein
was primarily concerned with the psychological dimension of the death
drive and saw the struggle between love and hate or life and death
drives as the origin of psychic development and mental functioning
(Klein, 1958). She used the death drive as a clinical concept in order
to make sense of aggressive and destructive phenomena encountered
in the consulting room. In her view, the workings of the death drive
were not silent or mute but could readily be observed and experienced
in clinical work with patients. For instance, the effects of the workings of the death drive could immediately be felt as anxiety: "I hold

that anxiety arises from the operation of the Death Instinct within the organism, is felt as fear of annihilation (death) and takes the form of fear of persecution" (Klein, 1946, p. 100). The fundamental annihilation anxiety caused by the death drive sets in motion various defence mechanisms like splitting and projective identification, whereby the death drive immediately becomes attached to the object, turning it into the primary representative of the death drive in the sense of a bad, persecuting object. Similarly, she used the concept of the death drive to account for the severity and cruelty of the archaic superego. Later on, she highlighted the intricate relation between the death drive and envy, conceived as a primitive, destructive force aimed at life and life-giving objects itself (Klein, 1957).

The Kleinian tradition has arguably provided the most fertile ground for the development of the death drive concept. Other important psychoanalysts in Great Britain rejected the idea of an inborn destructive tendency, e.g. Fairbairn, who viewed aggression as always secondary to frustration (Chessick, 1992), or Winnicott, who found the notion of the death drive to be "unacceptable" and "unnecessary" (Winnicott, 1965). The prominence given to the concept in the Kleinian school has sometimes been likened to a sort of "differentiating label," which in turn has led some authors to imply that not only scientific or clinical reasons were decisive in the adherence to it but also more ideological motivations (Armengou, 2009; Spillius, 1994). Nevertheless, the death drive has shown exceptional "explanatory and clinical usefulness" for many analysts working in the Kleinian tradition (Beland, 2008). Significant contributions include the work of Bion on "attacks on linking" and "arrogance" (Bion, 1958, 1959), Rosenfeld's concept of "destructive narcissism" (Rosenfeld, 1971), and articles by Segal (Segal, 1993) and Feldman (Feldman, 2000). All of these approaches share a turning away from debates about the facticity of the death drive towards a discussion of its applicability and usefulness (Danckwardt, 2011). Paradigmatically, Hanna Segal tried to formulate her theory on the conflict between life and death drives "in purely psychological terms," distinguishing two fundamental reactions in relation to the inevitable experience of needs: "One, to seek satisfaction for the needs: that is life-promoting and leads to object seeking, love, and eventually object concern. The other is the drive to annihilate the need, to annihilate the perceiving experiencing self, as well as anything that is perceived" (Segal, 1993, p. 55). Segal therefore unties the concept of the death drive from biology and positions it firmly in the field of object relations (Beland, 2008; Bell, 2015), primarily in the form of envy: "If the death instinct is a reaction to a disturbance produced by needs, the object is perceived both as disturbance, the creator of the need, and as the unique object, capable of disturbance removal. As such, the needed breast is hated and envied" (Segal, 1993, pp. 59–60). One of the difficulties in discerning the death drive that Freud had put forward was the impossibility to observe its workings in isolation from libidinal admixture: "one can suspect [. . .] that the two kinds of instinct seldom – perhaps never – appear in isolation from each other, but are alloyed with each other in varying and very different proportions and so become unrecognizable to our judgement" (Freud, 1930, p. 119). Segal in turn postulated that due to the advances in psychoanalytic technique and the broadening of the spectrum of patients treated by analysts it was now possible to "detect the operation of the death instinct in an almost pure form . . . rather than in fusion" (Segal, 1993, p. 56). This was mainly made possible by a new understanding of countertransference, which, in turn, is inseparable from the overall developments in analytic object relations theory. There is a constant process of projection and introjection between patient and analyst, whereby at one point the patient projects his death drive into the analyst, who then feels paralysis, despair, or aggression; at another time the analyst becomes the container for all impulses to live, leading to excessive protectiveness and concern. These descriptions seek to illustrate the experience-near usage of the concept of the death drive typical in the Kleinian tradition. While Kleinian analysts using the death drive in their theoretical and clinical work have repeatedly been attacked for their "dogmatic rigidity" (Kernberg, 1969) or their purely "phenomenological" or "metaphorical" use of the notion (Penot, 2017), there is widespread agreement even among adherents of other psychoanalytic schools that the Kleinian tradition has been able to provide some of the most poignant contributions to the analysis of destructive phenomena so prevalent in the consulting room and beyond (Kernberg, 2009; Mitchell, 1993). It can reasonably be argued that the adoption and development of the concept of the death drive contributed significantly to this achievement (Beland, 2008; Bell, 2015).

American psychoanalysis in the form of ego psychology predominantly rejected the notion of the death drive (Bergmann, 2011). The tone was set by Hartmann, Kris, and Loewenstein, who did not outwardly reject the idea but rather sidestepped a detailed discussion of what they considered primarily to be "biological speculations" of Freud. They emphasized the importance of a dualistic drive theory, but advocated an aggressive drive independent of Freud's original idea of the death drive (Hartmann, Kris, & Loewenstein, 1947). Subsequently, the notion of the death drive all but disappeared from the ego-psychological works in the following decades (Kernberg, 2009; Lazar & Erlich, 1996). However, the pluralization of psychoanalysis in the United States in recent decades has also meant that the reception of the death drive concept has diversified (Cooper, 2008). For example, Kernberg recently made a case for the importance of the idea of the death drive and the ensuing debates surrounding it: "The death drive runs deeply against more optimistic views of human nature, based on the assumption that if severe frustrations or trauma were absent in early development then aggression would not be a major human problem" (Kernberg, 2009, p. 1009). While rejecting the death drive in the Freudian sense as a fundamental force in every individual, he nevertheless found the concept to be clinically useful (Kernberg, 2009): phenomena like sadism and masochism, repetition compulsion, negative therapeutic reaction, suicide, and violent and destructive phenomena in groups and society at large provide ample evidence for a profound self-destructive potential in humanity. Kernberg wants to reserve the notion of the death drive to very severe cases of psychopathology, in which hateful aggressivity and perverse libidinization of aggressive tendencies dominate the clinical picture: "The death drive, I propose, is not a primary drive, but represents a significant complication of aggression as a major motivational system, is central in the therapeutic work with severe psychopathology, and as such is eminently useful as a concept in the clinical realm" (Kernberg, 2009, p. 1018).

French perspectives

In contrast to the predominantly clinical use of the concept of the death drive in the Kleinian tradition and in Kernberg's work, French psychoanalysts generally took a more theoretical or metapsychological approach. Besides Melanie Klein, Jacques Lacan was arguably the most influential analyst to embrace Freud's notion. While it is beyond the scope of this overview to do justice to the complex and sophisticated Lacanian interpretations of the death drive (cf. Ruhs, in this book), it is clear that Lacan regarded this concept as central to psychoanalysis: "For to evade the death instinct in his [Freud's] doctrine is not to know his doctrine at all" (Lacan, 1960, p. 679). He was careful to detach the death drive from any biological roots and initially tried to situate the self-destructive tendency designated by the death drive in the imaginary dimension of human existence and closely linked it to narcissistic phenomena and their emergence in the mirror stage. In the 1950s, under the influence of Saussure's linguistics and the structuralist ideas of Lévi-Strauss, Lacan rather saw the death instinct as being profoundly related to the phenomenon of language or the symbolic order (López, 1996). The signifier, as the "murder of the thing," introduces a fundamental negativity, a lack, into human existence: "The death instinct is only the mask of the symbolic order" (Lacan, 1954–55, p. 326). In his late teaching, Lacan finally relates the death drive to the dimension of the real in the form of *jouissance*, a form of excessive enjoyment that lies beyond the pleasure principle. Insofar as all drives strive toward *jouissance*, Lacan states that "every drive is virtually a death drive" (Lacan, 1966, p. 719). In short, the death drive was central to each of Lacan's conceptual innovations, though he was eventually led to question the dualistic foundation of Freudian drive theory. The binary opposition of life and the death drives as a form of metaphysical entities was also criticized by another leading French theoretician, Jean Laplanche (1976). For Laplanche, the struggle between life and death drives was not one between sexuality and non-sexual aggressivity, but rather was to be located internal to sexuality itself. Thus he reformulated the antagonism as one between the "sexual life and the sexual death drives" and respectively related them to the psychic mechanisms of binding and unbinding:

> Rather than two hypothetical biological forces, this opposition concerns two distinct mechanisms in the sphere of human fantasy: the bound (secondary) process and the unbound (primary) process. Or, more accurately, two principles: the principle of binding, which would introduce order for the sexual life drives, and the principle of unbinding, which takes its power from the sexual death drives.
>
> (Laplanche, 2004, p. 456)

Laplanche saw Freud's introduction of the death drive as primarily motivated by reasons internal to the development of his thinking and especially as an answer to the problems Freudian metapsychology was confronted with after the discovery of narcissism. For Laplanche, there are two tendencies of sexuality observable in Freud's theory: besides the anarchic and unbound sexuality of the "Three Essays on the Theory of Sexuality" (1905), there appears in the form of narcissism a bound and unitary form of sexuality related to the love of whole objects, with the ego as its first total object:

> In the face of the risk that a victorious, narcissistic Eros might take over completely, there arises – in real life, just as much as in the development of Freudian thought – an imperious need to re-affirm the drive in its most radical form: as something "demonic," obeying nothing but the primary process and the compulsions of fantasy. From this point of view, the so called death drive would be nothing but the re-establishment of the untamed dimension of sexuality.
>
> (Laplanche, 2004, p. 462)

Laplanche then grounds his ideas on the sexual life and death drives in his "general theory of seduction" and the primary importance of the message of the Other in the origin of psychic life. Without being able to further trace these developments here, Laplanche's thinking could in a way be seen as exemplary for the engagement with the notion of the death drive prevalent in French psychoanalysis. He takes the metapsychological aspects of the concept very seriously and is critical of simplistic and reductionist views, which in his opinion are dominant in the Kleinian tradition. Against the "Manichean" tendency of the Kleinian views of the death drive, he proposes an approach equating the drive antagonism with basic modes of psychic functioning: "Thus, in the grandiose opposition of life and death drives, there is nothing mysterious or metaphysical. In question are two principles, of binding and unbinding, whose opposition is at work on the inside of the psychical apparatus" (Laplanche, 2004, p. 465).

To a certain extent, these ideas find their repercussions in the work of André Green, who repeatedly addressed the debates surrounding the notion of the death drive in his writings (1999, 2002, 2007, 2010). Green also emphasized the importance of the mechanisms of unbinding and dissolution as primary manifestations of the death drive. He coined the term "disobjectalizing function" as the specific mode of action of the death drive in its opposition to the "objectalizing function" of the life drives (Green, 1999). The fundamental aim of the death drive is disinvestment and disengagement. In keeping with the central Freudian idea that the death drive primarily is directed towards the self and only subsequently turned outwards against the object in the form of aggression, Green sees the auto-destructive tendency as the primary exponent of the death drive. In its most radical form, it not only attacks the object or the relation to the object, but rather affects the ego or the very process of cathexis itself, leading to bland, impoverished mental functioning and devitalized and empty psychic states. For Green, this withdrawal of cathexis or the disobjectalizing function served to provide a model for the understanding of severe cases of psychopathology, such as suicidal depression or psychosis. He also related it to the ideas of the Paris Psychosomatic School with their concepts such as operative thought and essential depression. Furthermore, he also used the opposition of life and death drives as the framework for his differentiation between positive and negative forms of narcissism (Green, 2002).

Status quo

The discourses and developments previously outlined are broadly reflected in the most recent contributions to the debate as illustrated by a special educational section on the death drive in *The International Journal of Psychoanalysis* (April 2015). Claudia Frank's work on the history of the reception of the death drive in Germany has already been referred to (Frank, 2015). David Bell provides an overview of contemporary Kleinian perspectives on the death drive (2015). He suggests that the concept of the death drive is currently used in three phenomenologically different ways among Kleinians: the first one concerns violent acts of destruction, not only in the form of outward aggression but also an internal attack on thinking; the second one describes a seductive lure into mindlessness in the sense of Freud's Nirvana principle; and the third one is associated with the deadening prevention of development via the sadistic control and immobilization of the object. Notably, two of the three models are concerned with quiet, deadening processes, picking up the Freudian idea of the "mute" workings of the pure death drive. While Bell affirms the usefulness of the concept of the death drive, De Masi (2015), drawing on similar Kleinian sources, but also on Winnicott and attachment research, comes to a different conclusion and reasons that it is not necessary to suppose a primary, innate destructive force as captured by the death drive. He argues that the destructiveness encountered in the consulting room is better conceptualized as deriving from infantile trauma and the ensuing development of omnipotent pathological defensive structures against affective relationships and life itself (De Masi, 2015). Finally, in the same educational section of the *International Journal*, Falcao picks up the French metapsychological approach, especially Green's idea of the disobjectalizing function of the death drive, and tries to locate these processes in the transference-countertransference dynamic of the analytic situation (Falcao, 2015).

Without any pretence of completeness, the following threads can be observed in the contemporary debates about the death drive:

- A certain predominance of clinical approaches primarily concerned with the usefulness or applicability of the concept of the death drive, as opposed to questions about the existence or non-existence of it (Beland, 2008; Danckwardt, 2011; De Masi, 2015; Kernberg, 2009; Segal, 1993).
- A common "metaphorical use" of the concept, in which the term is used in a more pragmatic way to denote destructive tendencies, while leaving out many of the characteristics originally entailed in the concept, e.g. the status as a drive or its biological aspects (Bell, 2015; Feldman, 2000; Penot, 2017).
- An ongoing debate about the adequate conceptualization of aggression in its relation to the death drive with many authors arguing for a necessary differentiation between different types of aggression. The emphasis is on the clinical and metapsychological differentiation of aggression with the attendant rejection of the simplified idea of aggression as a direct expression of a destructive drive (De Masi, 2015; Kernberg, 2009; Laplanche, 2004; Roussillon, 2013).
- At the same time we can also note an opposing effort to take up and further develop the "quietistic" aspects of the death drive concept in order to draw attention to and elucidate more subtle deadening processes in the clinical work that are easily overlooked behind the "conspicuous and noisy" (Freud, 1930, p. 119) manifestations of Eros (Bell, 2015; Feldman, 2000; Schmidt-Hellerau, 1997).
- A renewed interest in metapsychological aspects related to the death drive with a special focus on the mechanism of unbinding and dissolution, which includes reflections on the constructive and structure-forming properties of the death drive (Danckwardt, 2011; Green, 1999, 2010; Laplanche, 2004; Penot, 2017; Rosenberg, 1991).

- This goes along with the widespread conviction that it is not possible to meaningfully discuss the death drive without always and at the same time taking into account the vicissitudes of its counterpart, Eros (Danckwardt, 2011, 2014; Laplanche, 2004).
- With a few notable exceptions, there is almost a complete absence of works by practicing analysts making use of the death drive for the purpose of a psychoanalytic understanding of cultural or societal phenomena in the tradition of Freud's "Civilization and its Discontents" (1930) and "Why War?" (1933b) (Green, 2010; Laub & Lee, 2003; Richard, 2011; Segal, 1997). On the other hand, philosophers or other social theorists, in a tradition going back to the Frankfurt School, still adopt the concept of the death drive for their analyses (Butler, 2014; Marcuse, 1955; Žižek, 2011).
- Finally, there is a decline in direct attacks or overt criticism of the concept, which might be understood as a product of the pluralization of the analytic world and the scarcity of serious controversies between the various groups or schools. This leads to the unchallenged continued use of the concept in some traditions and to its equally unquestioned rejection in other groups (Bernardi, 2002).

Where does this short overview of the trajectories of the concept of the death drive leave us today? Almost a hundred years after its introduction into psychoanalytic thinking, issues concerning the exact definition, the conceptual status, or even the very existence of this drive are still unresolved and potentially issues of debate. As mentioned, a rising interest in the death drive can be observed in recent years. A quick search of the Psychoanalytic Electronic Publishing (PEP) library indicates an increase in publications on the death drive from 27 articles between 1980–1999 to 60 papers between 2000–2018.[4] Beyond the important difficulties inherent in the notion of death drive, there seems to be an unremitting attraction of the idea as a "conceptual container" for the analysis of destructive, deadening, and dissolving processes that might otherwise escape adequate attention. Next to the "explanatory and clinical usefulness" (Beland, 2008) of a concept, its ability to generate further discourse and debate is also a crucial sign of the vitality and usefulness of an idea. In this sense, the notion of the death drive seems to be very alive. Contemporary psychoanalysis has reached a stage where conceptual uniformity is no longer possible. There is no generally accepted authority – be it a person or an institutional entity – that could determine the "true" nature of the death drive. It is therefore not surprising that there is an "absence of a unified notion of the death drive" (Armengou, 2009, p. 265). While conceptual obscurity and inaccuracy certainly constitute a problem for psychoanalysis (and any other science), a certain ambiguity and polysemy of a concept like the death drive might actually be considered to be a virtue. The death drive may thus be seen as a primary example of an "elastic concept," which plays an important part in holding psychoanalytic theory together and makes theoretical development without radical disruptions possible (Sandler, 1983). For better or worse, the only common reference point for psychoanalysis is the work of Sigmund Freud and while it is important to not fall into the traps of blind idolatry and uncritical partisanship, the continuous engagement with his foundational concepts might make debates and controversies between the heterogeneous psychoanalytic traditions possible.

Book overview

It was the idea of such a debate that led to the compilation of the present book, the aim of which is to provide an overview of contemporary perspectives on the topic of the death drive. Our book brings together contributions from different psychoanalytic traditions and elucidates their respective understanding of the death drive. The original idea for this volume was born at a conference of the International Psychoanalytical Studies Organization (IPSO) held in Vienna in July 2016. This colloquium was organized as a series of debates between senior analysts of the two IPA-affiliated societies in Austria (Vienna Psychoanalytic Society and Vienna Psychoanalytic Association). These debates addressed aspects and manifestations of the death drive in in three areas of psychoanalytic thought: theory, clinic, and culture. The success of the conference and the richness of the discussions it engendered gave rise to the present volume, which brings together a collection of revised and adapted papers presented at the colloquium.

The first part of the volume deals with theoretical aspects of the death drive from three different perspectives. Hemma Rössler-Schülein provides a contemporary Kleinian perspective on the death drive, Friedl Früh rereads Freud's "Beyond the Pleasure Principle" from a viewpoint influenced by Laplanche, and Jeanne Wolff Bernstein offers a detailed account of the place of the death drive in Freud's theory and its influence on Lacan's

concept of *jouissance*. The second part of this volume focuses on manifestations of the death drive in clinical work. Sylvia Zwettler-Otte and Fritz
Lackinger discuss case vignettes as well as literary examples (Schnitzler) to
demonstrate various aspects of the death drive that are important for psychoanalytic clinical work. The next part explores the workings of the death
drive in contemporary culture and society. Elisabeth Skale's contribution
takes Freud's "Civilization and Its Discontents" as a starting point and
investigates the unbinding and dissolving properties of the death drive
at work in modern-day cultural phenomena. The chapter by August Ruhs
uses a Lacanian understanding of the death drive to analyse social developments and the process of artistic creation and sublimation.

A final part is concerned with the specific history of psychoanalysis
in Austria and its interrelation with the concept of the death drive. First,
Daru Huppert explores the disruptive history of psychoanalysis in
Vienna in light of the death drive. Then, Thomas Aichhorn, Nadja Pakesch, and Tjark Kunstreich present findings from the working group
on the history of psychoanalysis of the Vienna Psychoanalytic Society,
which focuses on the forced emigration of Viennese psychoanalysts in
1938 and provides original research on the fate of several candidates of
the Society of the time.

In conclusion, the present book aims to provide an overview of the
current psychoanalytic understanding of the death drive with contributions from most major psychoanalytic traditions. It seeks to contribute
to the rekindled debate on the nature of human destructiveness and
hopefully will serve as a reference point for future conceptual developments in the field.

Notes

1   The term "death drive" is used as a translation for the German "*Todes-
    trieb*" throughout the introduction as opposed to Strachey's use of
    "death instinct" in the Standard Edition. Regarding the issue of transla-
    tion, cf. Zwettler-Otte (in this book).
2   Besides the highly problematic approach of biographical reductionism,
    many of the alleged personal factors are disproven on a factual level,
    e.g. the time of Sophie's death in relation to the development of the
    manuscript of "Beyond the Pleasure Principle" (cf. May, 2015).

3   Of course, the same holds true for many other psychoanalytic theories (Bernardi, 2002).
4   English-language publications with "death drive" or "death instinct" in the title.

References

Armengou, F. G. (2009). The death drive: Conceptual analysis and relevance in the Spanish psychoanalytic community. *The International Journal of Psychoanalysis, 90*:263–289.

Beland, H. (2008). Erklärungs-und Arbeitswert der Todestriebhypothese. Diskussion anhand klinischer und theoretischer Beispiele [The explanatory and clinical usefulness of the concept of death instinct: Discussion of clinical and theoretical examples of some of its representatives]. *Jahrbuch der Psychoanalyse, 56*:23–47.

Bell, D. L. (2015). The death drive: Phenomenological perspectives in contemporary Kleinian theory. *The International Journal of Psychoanalysis, 96*:411–423.

Bergmann, M. S. (2011). The dual impact of Freud's death and Freud's death instinct theory on the history of psychoanalysis. *Psychoanalytic Review, 98*:665–686.

Bernardi, R. (2002). The need for true controversies in psychoanalysis: The debates on Melanie Klein and Jacques Lacan in the Rio de la Plata. *The International Journal of Psychoanalysis, 83*:851–873.

Bion, W. R. (1958). On arrogance. *The International Journal of Psychoanalysis, 39*:144–146.

Bion, W. R. (1959). Attacks on linking. *The International Journal of Psychoanalysis, 40*:308–315.

Brun, R. (1953). Über Freuds Hypothese vom Todestrieb: Eine kritische Untersuchung [Freud's hypothesis concerning the death instinct: A critical study]. *Psyche – Zeitschrift für Psychoanalyse, 7*:81–111.

Butler, J. (2014). *Politik des Todestriebes. Der Fall Todesstrafe*. Vienna: Turian und Kant.

Chessick, R. D. (1992). The death instinct revisited. *Journal of the American Academy of Psychoanalysis, 20*:3–28.

Cooper, A. M. (2008). American psychoanalysis today: A plurality of orthodoxies. *Journal of the American Academy of Psychoanalysis and Dynamic Psychiatry, 36*:235–253.

Danckwardt, J. F. (2011). Die Verleugnung des Todestriebs [The denial of the death instinct]. *Jahrbuch der Psychoanalyse, 62*:137–163.

Danckwardt, J. F. (2014). Von Jenseits des Lustprinzips zur Banalität des Bösen: Weitere Bruchstücke zu Sigmund Freuds Lebens-Todestriebhypothese [From "Beyond the pleasure principle" to "the banality of evil": Further fragments concerning Sigmund Freud's hypothesis of life-and-death instincts]. *Jahrbuch der Psychoanalyse, 68*:219–249.

De Bianchedi, E. T., Antar, R., Fernández Bravo De Podetti, M. R., Grassano De Píccolo, E., Miravent, I., Pistiner De Cortiñas, L., Scalozub De Boschan, L. T., & Waserman, M. (1984). Beyond Freudian metapsychology: The metapsychological points of view of the Kleinian school. *The International Journal of Psychoanalysis, 65*:389–398.

De Masi, F. (2015). Is the concept of the death drive still useful in the clinical field. *The International Journal of Psychoanalysis, 96*:445–458.

Ekstein, R. (1949). A biographical comment on Freud's dual instinct theory. *American Imago, 6*:211–216.

Falcao, L. (2015). Death drive, destructive drive and the desobjectalizing function in the analytic process. *The International Journal of Psychoanalysis, 96*:459–476.

Feldman, M. (2000). Some views on the manifestation of the death instinct in clinical work. *The International Journal of Psychoanalysis, 81*:53–65.

Frank, C. (2015). On the reception of the concept of the death drive in Germany: Expressing and resisting an "evil principle"? *The International Journal of Psychoanalysis, 96*:425–444.

Freud, S. (1905). *Three Essays on the Theory of Sexuality*. Standard Edition 7:123–246.

Freud, S. (1920). *Beyond the Pleasure Principle*. Standard Edition 18:1–64.

Freud, S. (1924). *The Economic Problem of Masochism*. Standard Edition 19:155–170.

Freud, S. (1925). *An Autobiographical Study*. Standard Edition 20:7–74.

Freud, S. (1930). *Civilization and Its Discontents*. Standard Edition 21:57–146.

Freud, S. (1933a). *New Introductory Lectures on Psycho-Analysis*. Standard Edition 22:1–182.

Freud, S. (1933b). *Why War?* Standard Edition 22:195–216.

Freud, S. (1937). *Analysis Terminable and Interminable*. Standard Edition 23:209–254.

Freud, S. (1940 [1938]). *An Outline of Psycho-Analysis*. Standard Edition 23:139–208.

Green, A. (1999). *The Work of the Negative*. London: Free Association.

Green, A. (2002). A dual conception of narcissism: Positive and negative organizations. *Psychoanalytic Quarterly*, 71:631–649.

Green, A. (2007). The death drive: Meaning, objections, substitutes. In: D. Birksted-Breen, S. Flanders & A. Gibeault (Eds.), *Reading French Psychoanalysis* (pp. 496–515). London: Routledge, 2010.

Green, A. (2010). *Pourquoi les pulsions de destruction ou de mort?* Paris: Ithaque.

Hanly, C. (1990). The concept of truth in psychoanalysis. *The International Journal of Psychoanalysis*, 71:375–383.

Hartmann, H., Kris, E., & Loewenstein, R. M. (1947). Notes on the theory of aggression. *The Psychoanalytic Study of the Child*, 3:9–36.

Jones, E. (1957). *Sigmund Freud Life and Work (Volume Three: The Last Phase 1919–1939)*. London: The Hogarth Press.

Kernberg, O. F. (1969). A contribution to the ego-psychological critique of the Kleinian school. *The International Journal of Psychoanalysis*, 50:317–333.

Kernberg, O. F. (2009). The concept of the death drive: A clinical perspective. *The International Journal of Psychoanalysis*, 90:1009–1023.

King, P., & Steiner, R. (Eds.) (1991). *The Freud-Klein Controversies 1941–45*. London: Routledge.

Klein, M. (1946). Notes on some schizoid mechanisms. *The International Journal of Psychoanalysis*, 27:99–110.

Klein, M. (1957). Envy and gratitude. In: *Envy and Gratitude: And Other Works, 1946–1963* (pp. 176–235). London: The Hogarth Press and the Institute of Psycho-Analysis, 1975.

Klein, M. (1958). On the development of mental functioning. *The International Journal of Psychoanalysis*, 39:84–90.

Lacan, J. (1954–55). *The Ego in Freud's Theory and in the Technique of Psychoanalysis (The Seminar of Jacques Lacan, Book II)*. New York: WW Norton, 1988.

Lacan, J. (1960). The subversion of the subject and the dialectic of desire in the Freudian unconscious. In: *Ecrits: The First Complete Edition in English* (pp. 671–702). New York: WW Norton, 2006.

Lacan, J. (1966). Position of the unconscious. In: *Ecrits: The First Complete Edition in English* (pp. 703–721). New York: WW Norton, 2006.

Laplanche, J. (1976). *Life and Death in Psychoanalysis*. Baltimore: Johns Hopkins University.

Laplanche, J. (2004). The so-called "death drive": A sexual drive. *British Journal of Psychotherapy*, 20:455–471.

Laub, D., & Lee, S. (2003). Thanatos and massive psychic trauma: The impact of the death instinct on knowing, remembering, and forgetting. *Journal of the American Psychoanalytic Association*, 51:433–464.

Lazar, R., & Erlich, H. S. (1996). Repetition compulsion: A reexamination of the concept and the phenomenon. *Psychoanalysis and Contemporary Thought*, *19*:29–55.

López, D. B. (1996). The enigma of the death drive: A revisiting. *Psychoanalysis and Contemporary Thought*, *19*:3–27.

Marcuse, H. (1955). *Eros and Civilization: A Philosophical Inquiry into Freud*. Boston: Beacon Press.

May, U. (2015). The third step in drive theory: On the genesis of "Beyond the Pleasure Principle". *Psychoanalysis and History*, *17*:205–272.

Mitchell, S. A. (1993). Aggression and the endangered self. *Psychoanalytic Quarterly*, *62*:351–382.

Penot, B. (2017). The so-called death drive, an indispensable force for any subjective life. *The International Journal of Psychoanalysis*, *98*:299–321.

Richard, F. (2011). Les formes actuelles du malaise dans la culture. *Recherches en psychanalyse*, *11*:6–17.

Rosenberg, B. (1991). *Masochisme mortifère et masochisme gardien de la vie*. Paris: Presses universitaires de France.

Rosenfeld, H. (1971). A clinical approach to the psychoanalytic theory of the life and death instincts: An investigation into the aggressive aspects of narcissism. *The International Journal of Psychoanalysis*, *52*:169–178.

Roussillon, R. (2013). The function of the object in the binding and unbinding of the drives. *The International Journal of Psychoanalysis*, *94*:257–276.

Sandler, J. (1983). Reflections on some relations between psychoanalytic concepts and psychoanalytic practice. *The International Journal of Psychoanalysis*, *64*:35–45.

Schmidt-Hellerau, C. (1997). Libido and lethe: Fundamentals of a formalised conception of metapsychology. *The International Journal of Psychoanalysis*, *78*:683–697.

Schmidt-Hellerau, C. (2005). We are driven. *Psychoanalytic Quarterly*, *74*:989–1028.

Segal, H. (1993). On the clinical usefulness of the concept of death instinct. *The International Journal of Psychoanalysis*, *74*:55–61.

Segal, H. (1997). *Psychoanalysis, Literature, and War: Papers, 1972–1995*. London: Routledge.

Spillius, E. B. (1994). Developments in Kleinian thought: Overview and personal view. *Psychoanalytic Inquiry*, *14*:324–364.

Winnicott, D. W. (1965). *The Maturational Processes and the Facilitating Environment: Studies in the Theory of Emotional Development*. London: The Hogarth Press and the Institute of Psycho-Analysis.

Žižek, S. (2011). *Living in the End Times*. New York: Verso.

PART I
THEORY

CHAPTER 1

The struggle between good and evil: The concept of the death drive from a Kleinian perspective

Hemma Rössler-Schülein

Introduction

This chapter focuses on applications of the death drive theory in the Kleinian psychoanalytic tradition. This body of knowledge was mainly developed in the English-speaking world and by analysts forced to emigrate from Austria and Germany following the outbreak of World War II. Therefore, it might be interesting to begin discussing this concept by briefly referring to the difficulties entailed in the translation of the German term "Trieb" into English. In a speech recorded by the BBC in December 1938, Sigmund Freud referred to the *role of instinctual urges*. Several other psychoanalysts, beginning in the 1930s with Stevens (1930) and Lampl-De Groot (1933), prefer "drive" instead of "instinct" or use both terms synonymously (Jekels & Bergler, 1940). In his paper "The Drive to Amass Wealth," Fenichel (1938) cautions against the tendency to closely link the theory of neuroses or those about social institutions to our understanding of biological instincts, despite the fact that psychoanalysis may have taught us to highly value the role of concrete, as in physical, infantile experience. Along similar lines, Hanna Segal felt it was both possible and desirable to formulate the conflict between the life and death instincts in purely psychological terms. She adds in a footnote: "I have always disagreed with the translation of Trieb as 'instinct.' I agree with Bettelheim that the best translation is the French 'pulsion.' The nearest in English would be 'drive'" (Segal, 1993, p. 55). Kernberg (2001) made this distinction even clearer: he pointed out that in contrast to the innate and inalterable nature of instincts, drives have an essentially psychic nature; they are continuous, individualized, and are subject to modification through displacement or condensation throughout development.

The preference for the term "death drive" in the Kleinian tradition underscores how life and death drives constitute powerful ever-present psychological processes or forces in the mind. This approach is based on clinical experience and tries to minimize terminological ambiguity by stressing the psychological character of the death drive and by avoiding simplistic biological equivocation.

Starting points from Freud's theory

In his third theory of drives Freud embarked on a reformulation of his ideas based on explorations of phenomena encountered in clinical work such as repetitive processes in traumatic neuroses, sadism and masochism, the melancholic superego, and the negative therapeutic reaction. In addition, he sought to understand societal phenomena such as war and populism from a psychoanalytic perspective. Possibly, the idea of the death instinct was influenced by the experiences and trauma of World War I (Jones, 1957, pp. 41–43; Laub & Lee, 2003).

Freud tried to understand why people tend to repeat painful or traumatic experiences, since such behaviour struck him as contradictory to the "pleasure principle." In line with the idea that "the aim of all life is death" (Freud, 1920, p. 38), and seeking to resolve this contradiction, he formulated the idea of the death instinct in his work "Beyond the Pleasure Principle" (1920). There, the death instinct was described as a compulsion to reproduce the very experience of chaos and trauma. Freud described this inner dynamic as an instinct that operates silently and unobtrusively and as "an urge inherent in organic life to restore an earlier state of things" (Freud, 1920, p. 36). The ultimate goal of this instinct is "to return to the quiescence of the inorganic world" (Freud, 1920, p. 62). When the "earlier state of things" is chaotic or traumatic, the urge to restore ends up operating as a force of traumatic repetition.

This text can be regarded as a turning point in Freud's thinking about the workings of the mind, yet it raised several theoretical questions. Subsequently, Freud tried to situate the dualistic drive concept in relation to the conflict between the instances of the id, the ego, and the superego. He thought the link was the guilt-consciousness characteristic of melancholia that he equated with the domination of the superego by the death instinct: "What is now holding sway in the super-ego is, as it were, a pure culture of the death instinct, and in fact it often enough succeeds in driving the ego into death, if the latter does not fend off its tyrant in time by the change round into mania" (Freud, 1923, p. 53). Nonetheless, instinctual fusion remained hard to grasp. In the 1924 paper "The Economic Problem of Masochism," Freud talked about moral masochism as "a classical piece of evidence for the existence of 'instinctual fusion': its dangerousness lies in its origin in the death instinct and represents that part of the latter which escaped deflection on to the outer world in the form of an instinct of destruction" (Freud, 1924, p. 170). In later texts, Freud (1930, 1937) spoke of aggression as the "descendant and chief representative" of the death drive. Besides talking about a primary form of destructiveness, which tends to dissolve units and is present right from the beginning of life, he also reflected about the fate of aggression that is either deflected outwards or bound by the superego and about the resulting relations between ego and superego.

> It might be assumed that the death instinct operated silently *within the organism towards its dissolution, but that, of course, was no proof. A more fruitful idea was that a portion of the instinct is diverted towards the external world and comes to light as an instinct of aggressiveness and destructiveness.* In this way the instinct itself could be pressed into the service of Eros, in that the organism was destroying some other thing, whether animate or inanimate, instead of destroying its own self.
>
> (Freud, 1930, p. 118, *own italics*)

Freud also used the theory of the death instinct to further his understanding of deep-seated resistances against analytic treatment. The negative therapeutic reaction is an indication of a deep-seated unconscious resistance that comes from the superego, or, more precisely, from specific relations between ego and superego. By linking this resistance to the death instinct, Freud takes a step further and elevates this resistance into something much bigger:

> One portion of this force has been recognized by us, undoubtedly with justice, as the sense of guilt and need for punishment, and has been localized by us in the ego's relation to the super-ego. But this is only the portion of it which is, as it were, psychically bound by the super-ego and thus becomes recognizable; other quotas of the same force, bound or free, may be at work in other, unspecified places. If we take into consideration the total picture made up of the phenomena of masochism immanent in so many people, the negative therapeutic reaction and the sense of guilt found in so many neurotics, we shall no longer be able to adhere to the belief that mental events are exclusively governed by the desire for pleasure. These phenomena are unmistakable indications of the presence of a power in mental life which we call the *instinct of aggression or of destruction according to its aims, and which we trace back to the original death instinct of living matter*.
>
> (Freud, 1937, pp. 242–243, *own italics*)

Insofar as it is derived from the death instinct, the negative therapeutic reaction is rooted in the economy of psychic life. More specifically, guilt represents the workings of that portion of the death instinct that is psychically bound by the superego. Loewald (1972) explains that the aggressive share of the superego, which is composed of the aggressive forces of the introjected oedipal imagos and the subject's aggressive impulses, constitutes a structured representative of the death instinct, while other portions of it manifest themselves in ways that seem analytically inaccessible since they have not attained definitive or circumscribed psychic representation.

Melanie Klein's "evil principle" and subsequent adoption of the notion of the death drive

The use and application of the concept of the death instinct was at the centre of debates between the Vienna and British Societies from early on. Melanie Klein and her followers were particularly interested in the fate of the superego and that of incorporated objects. Isaacs firmly stated that Melanie Klein's views on the concept of the death drive were not only derived from Freud's own theories and observations but in

large parts were identical with his. "Where they differ they are a necessary development of his work" (King & Steiner, 1991, p. 377). In this
regard, it may be helpful to remember how Freud himself dealt with
new theoretical findings. When revising his drive theory for the first
time he pointed to the significance of clinical observation: "For these
ideas are not the foundation of science, upon which everything rests:
that foundation is observation alone. They are not the bottom but the
top of the whole structure, and they can be replaced and discarded
without damaging it" (Freud, 1914, p. 77).

Melanie Klein developed her ideas on the basis of observations made
in the course of psychoanalytic work with children. The so-called evil
principle first made its appearance in November 1925 in the discussion
of the six-year-old obsessional neurotic girl called Erna.

In a careful reconstruction of the case of Erna, Claudia Frank and
Heinz Weiss (1996) show how Melanie Klein intuitively arrived at her
theoretical formulation of destructive phenomena. In Erna's drawings,
the evil principle is represented by a witch who regularly takes on the
characteristics of the good princess or vice versa. Eventually the two
opposing figures come to resemble each other. In one specific narrative,
at the sound of a thunderbolt the ugly figure repeatedly turns into the
beautiful one and the beautiful one into the ugly one. This demonstrates
quite vividly the unsuccessful endeavour to integrate the two parts of
the little girl's personality, the splitting arising "out of the necessity to
ward off the evil principle" (cited in Frank, 2009, p. 178). Claudia Frank
(2011) points out that Melanie Klein's formulation captures important
characteristics: there is something in oneself that is "completely evil"
and which feels like an impersonal power (or "principle") that cannot simply be warded off. There is a struggle between the opposing
tendencies aiming at the "dissolution of the context," in this case the
"decomposition into two parts of the personality," as opposed to the
attempts to form one "larger unity, in an effort to keep the two parts
together, to connect and to merge somehow" (Frank, 2011, pp. 81–82,
own translation).

Klein may not have fully realized the value of her discovery at the
time, making no further use of the concept of the evil principle (Frank,
2015, p. 431). However, in her clinical practice she continued to address
the manifestations of a harsh and punishing superego, the vicious
circle between aggression causing anxiety again enhancing aggression, and the interplay between internal and external factors in early

development. In an effort to accommodate her findings within Freud's theoretical framework, she finally adopted Freud's concept of the death drive. In 1932 she wrote:

> In that early phase of development which I have termed the phase of maximal sadism, I have found that all the pre-genital stages and the genital stage as well are cathected in rapid succession. What then happens is that the libido enters upon a struggle with the destructive impulses and gradually consolidates its positions. Side by side with the polarity of the life-instinct and the death-instinct we may, I think, place their interaction as a fundamental factor in the dynamic processes of the mind. There is an indissoluble bond between the libido and the destructive tendencies which puts the former to a great extent in the power of the latter. But the vicious circle dominated by the death-instinct, in which aggression gives rise to anxiety and anxiety reinforces aggression, can be broken through by the libidinal forces when these have gained in strength. As we know, in the early stages of development the life-instinct has to exert its power to the utmost in order to maintain itself against the death-instinct. But this very necessity stimulates the growth of the sexual life of the individual.
>
> (Klein, 1932, pp. 211–212)

By depicting the experience of the struggle between love and hate as a normal, albeit frightening ambivalence inherent in all relations, it quickly became evident to Melanie Klein that the death instinct is an opponent of libidinal forces, just like the so-called evil principle. The anxieties associated with this struggle are a major topic throughout her work. In 1946, Klein described some problems of the early ego, claiming it lacked cohesiveness. The ego's tendency towards integration alternates with a tendency towards disintegration. Anxiety arising from the operation of the death instinct within the organism is felt as fear of annihilation (death) and takes the form of fear of persecution. The fear of the destructive impulse attaches itself to an object and is experienced as fear of an uncontrollable overpowering object. Other important sources of primary anxiety are the trauma of birth (separation anxiety) and the frustration of bodily needs. These experiences too are felt to be caused by bad objects. Furthermore, even if these objects are thought to be external, they become internal persecutors through introjection, thus reinforcing the fear of the destructive impulse within. The vital need to deal with anxiety forces the early ego to develop primary mechanisms and defences. The destructive impulse is partly projected outwards (deflection of the death instinct) and attaches itself at once to the primary external object, the mother's breast. In line with Freud, Klein argued that the remaining portion of the destructive impulse is bound by the libido within the organism. However, neither of these processes entirely fulfils their purpose, and therefore the anxiety of being destroyed from within remains active. Under the pressure of this threat the ego tends to fall to bits due to its lack of cohesiveness. This falling to bits underlies states of disintegration in schizophrenics.

Comparing Freud's and Klein's use of the death drive concept

According to Freud, primary destructiveness involves the fusion of life and death instincts. In turn, aggressiveness involves the turning of the fused instincts outwards. Klein, too, thinks that the death instinct is projected outwards into external objects, but she is of the opinion that this additionally involves splitting: both good from bad internal objects, and good from bad parts of the self. According to Klein, insofar as the struggle between the two instincts is operative from the very beginning of life, this also explains why there is an ego from birth onwards (Klein, 1958, p. 246). The mastery of anxiety is one of the ego's main functions. The primitive ego experiences this anxiety as a threat of annihilation from within. In defence, it projects it outwards onto and into objects. Freud talks of this process in more abstract terms: it is the organism (rather than the ego) that deflects (rather than projects) the death instinct outwards into objects.

Unlike Freud, Klein thinks that the unconscious contains a representation of death which coincides with the representation of bad and persecutory objects (Blass, 2014). The primitive superego, which in the internal world threatens the infant with death, constitutes one of the earliest representations of the death instinct. If this were to remain unmodified, the bad objects would produce the experience of inner death. In her later work, Klein came to view envy as the clearest manifestation of the death instinct. Envy is intractable because it motivates attacks of the good object thus spoiling and depleting the ego's internal and external resources. It interferes with the basic and early splitting of good object from bad, and of good aspects of the self from bad ones. Since differentiation and, later, integration depend on the successful development of these early splitting processes, envy is a severe obstacle to development and is heavily defended against (Spillius, 1983).

With "On the Development of Mental Functioning" (1958), Klein made a new turn with regard to her conception of the superego. The earliest and most threatening inner objects are no longer part of the superego, but located in a separate area, split from the ego and superego. This is the "deep unconscious" (Klein, 1975, p. 332) that remains unintegrated and unchanged. From here, these objects become sources of acute anxiety that can infiltrate and overwhelm the ego (Klein, 1975, p. 334). The emergence of the superego is conceptualized as a process through which the ego (strengthened by the internalization of the good object and identification with it) projects a part of the death instinct into the part split by the ego. Likewise, a part of the life instinct is distracted, so that good and evil objects are separated from the ego into the superego. Through integration, the death drive as bound by the superego is projected into the frustrating mother. The death drive affects the good objects of the superego, its prohibitions and injuries triggering fear (Klein, 1958, p. 240). The superego, insofar as it is bound with the good object and even strives for its preservation, comes close to the actual good mother. It is especially the early superego, which contains unfused life and death instincts, that is extremely harsh and persecuting. An overwhelming superego, almost indistinguishable from destructive impulses and internal persecutors, plays an important part in the psychopathological processes in schizophrenics.

Both Freud und Klein emphasized the self-destructive consequence of a sadistic superego and used this to explain the psychopathology of suicidal depression. Under the influence of self-destructive impulses, what is sought is not "nirvana" but rather the active destruction of libidinal relations with significant others. A destructive life-hating force assumes the upper hand in some patients and can induce psychosis. The Kleinian concept of the inner world describes a largely unconscious subjective experience of ego and objects, good and bad, built up through the constant operation of splitting, projection, and introjection. Even though Klein mentions the re-introjection of objects or parts of objects that were previously projected outwards, she does not go into detail as to what happens to these objects in the internal world, nor about whether and how the ego identifies with bad internal objects.

The organization of the death instinct in pathological character formation

Later authors in the Kleinian tradition sought to complete the preceding picture of the internal world by exploring narcissistic identification processes, both projective and introjective ones, as distinct from identifications that allow varying measures of separateness of internal objects and the self.

Donald Meltzer expounded the idea of an internal pathological organization based on idealization of a bad self (Meltzer, 1968). In Meltzer's view, the destructive part of the personality aims to create confusion and chaos so that the good infantile self will abandon psychic and external reality, thus willingly submitting to the voluptuous despair offered by the bad self. Similar ideas were developed by Herbert Rosenfeld a few years later. Rosenfeld (1971)[1] demonstrated the pull towards death in self-destructive patients who wish to annihilate all experience of living in search of a state without pain or pleasure. In describing destructive narcissism, he postulates that in certain severe psychopathologies a bad internal entity or bad self is idealized. This pathological nucleus removes the subject from contact with emotions and from relating to others. The sick part, which is idealized, progressively comes to hold sway over the rest of the personality, using propaganda that promises an easy solution to every problem. This structure resembles a delusional object whose healthy parts tend to allow themselves to be captured. In this way, pain or doubts completely disappear and the subject is free to indulge in phantasy in any transgressive and pleasurable activity. These patients' destructive narcissism is organized in the same way as a criminal gang dominated by aggression and seeking to increase their destructiveness. A pathological superego allied to the sick part of the personality is often present. For this reason, blind obedience is demanded, and any insubordination is punished by attacks and intimidating accusations by a revengeful and judgemental superego. Therefore, this psychopathological organization cannot be regarded as a mere expression of the mechanisms of primitive aggression but represents a pathological distortion of psychic development and an idealization of a sick part of the self. Its supremacy results from the perverse transformation of the superego. As a result, destructiveness appears innocent and exciting (De Masi, 2015). The protective side of this figure is deceitful. As the patient tries to escape its domination, the psychotic organization threatens with retaliation, thus disclosing its delinquent nature (Meltzer, 1968; Rosenfeld, 1971). In very severe cases, the healthy part manages to contain the destructive part for some time, until the sick part starts to colonize the healthy part. The latter is weakened and cannot contain the sick part any longer. At this point diffusion occurs, that is to say, the death instinct (the sick part) becomes autonomous from the life instinct (the healthy part). The clinical aim is to rescue the libidinal self and help the patient become aware of the destructive omnipotence of the bad part of him. Once exposed, there is some hope that the bad self will be deflated and reveal itself as a "poor devil" instead of "The Devil."

This approach was further developed by De Masi (2015), who stresses the importance of early or repeated emotional trauma in the development of such pathology. He states that human destructiveness does not derive from an original availability (the death instinct) but needs a long and complex development and is sometimes prompted by environmental destructiveness. In this regard, it seems essential to assume the existence of an internal pathological organization that forms gradually and tends to conquer the mind, as elaborated by Rosenfeld. The transformative process favouring the construction of an inhuman world takes place in a state of mind that is dissociated from the rest of the personality. In this psychic retreat, destructiveness gives rise to a mental excitation that makes evil pleasurable and irresistible. De Masi makes an important clarification: whereas aggression is exhausted once the aim of lowering tension has been accomplished, destructiveness, sustained as it is by pleasure, tends to be self-perpetuating. Thus, human destructiveness is very strongly linked to pleasure that gets satisfaction from evil. To achieve this goal, and for primal aggressiveness to be transformed into destructiveness, a long process is required. In this process the innate resources are combined with the environmental causes to get to a perverse constellation that enhances the destructive act as evidence of power, superiority, and omnipotence. De Masi further explains:

> Some patients use psychic withdrawal as an alternative to experiences that serve to maintain contact with reality and mental growth. The use of the perceptive organs to create artificial states of well-being is what chiefly characterizes these states, rather than projection towards the world or curiosity. The fantasized construction of virtual and parallel

worlds wields a highly seductive power that prevents the patient from recognizing its pathogenic nature.

(2015, p. 456)

The omnipresence of life and death instinct in the consulting room

The application of the concept for describing difficulties with the experience of need in daily clinical practice was convincingly presented by Hanna Segal (1993; Steiner, 2015). Following Melanie Klein, Segal understood and used the concept of the death drive psychologically.

> One could formulate the conflict between the life and death instinct in purely psychological terms. Birth confronts us with the experience of needs. In relation to that experience there can be two reactions, and both, I think, are invariably present in all of us, though in varying proportions. One, to seek satisfaction for the needs: that is life-promoting and leads to object seeking, love, and eventually object concern. The other is the drive to annihilate the need, to annihilate the perceiving experiencing self, as well as anything that is perceived.
>
> (Segal, 1993, p. 55)

Segal emphasizes that the death instinct has meaning only in relation to and in perpetual conflict with the life instinct. These two great primordial forces not only oppose each other, they also tend to stimulate one another. If one gains a notable advantage the other is provoked into action. The death instinct can take the guise of a seductive pull towards death presented as a pain-free solution. Another manifestation is the patient's hatred of reality. This hatred and its replacement by omnipotent phantasy is one of two possible reactions to states of need. One is life-seeking and object-seeking, leading to an attempt to satisfy those needs in the real world, if necessary by aggressive striving. By contrast, destructiveness towards objects represents a deflection of self-destructiveness to the outside as described by Freud. Moreover, the wish to annihilate ends up directed against both the perceiving self and the object perceived. The part of the self that is capable of experiencing pain is attacked and the patient turns to omnipotent phantasy for gratification instead of relying on reality. Hanna Segal was particularly concerned with illustrating the conflict and mutual interaction between the two basic instincts. She also described the terrible negativity, an almost tangible deadliness, that can pervade an individual's life and become manifest as a state of awful despair (Segal, 1993; Steiner, 2015).

Segal emphasized that the conflict between life and death instincts is present in all of us. Like Klein, she considers that envy is suffused with the death instinct, although she criticized Klein for making the equation of envy and death instinct all too simple. One consequence of this connection might be a negative therapeutic reaction, in which envy and the fear of being envied dominates as a response to clinical improvement. A critical difficulty in the analysis of envy lies in the fact that it is such an unbearable experience that it has to be split off and projected onto others. Therefore, in many cases it becomes evident as a fear of being envied. Segal recognized that envy is universal and cannot be evaded, however she thought that it could be understood and worked through. As a result, the patient may become less compulsively forced to deal with it by evacuative projection. Envy may then be integrated where it can be modified by constructive elements associated with the life instinct. Moves towards integration can be thought of as representations of the life instinct and are opposed by fragmentation in the service of the death instinct. This emphasis forces us to recognize that disintegration and fragmentation are as much part of life as are the opposing tendencies to create structure and difference.

Feldman (2000) further investigated "the activities of spoiling and undermining" as manifestations of the death instinct in clinical work. These are manifested by way of attacking meaning, specificity and differences thus retarding or undermining developmental processes. Feldman writes: "The vitality is taken out of the patient himself and his objects, and although in an important sense these drives are 'anti-life . . .', their aim is not literally to kill or to annihilate, but to maintain a link with the object that often has a tormenting quality." (Feldman, 2000, p. 64). The gratification bound up in these manifestations is the source of their frequently compulsive quality. However, this gratification does not result from fusion with the life instinct. Rather, sexuality and sexual excitement are recruited or "hijacked" by the death instinct to serve its purposes: "the gratification obtained from attacking, spoiling, and undermining, whether directed at the self or the object, is an essential element of such a destructive drive." (Feldman, 2000, p.64) These phenomena are closely related to those that led Klein to recognize the importance of envy as a destructive force.

Attempts and difficulties of integration

The clinical application of Freud's theory of the death drive within the Kleinian tradition kept the concept alive and helped develop it further. Derived usages of the concept cover a wide range of phenomena such as fear of annihilation, terror of disintegration, primitive envy, pathological character formations, pleasure in destructiveness, anti-life and anti-object relational force, and attack against the perceiving self. It is not always easy to integrate all these concepts and bring them under a common denominator. There remains a lack of uniformity and a certain uncertainty (Spillius et al., 2011).

An attempt at clarification at the phenomenological level was made by David Bell (2015), who based his analysis on the applications of the concept by Bion, Britton, Feldman, Joseph, and Segal. Accordingly, he differentiates three models of the death drive in contemporary Kleinian theory. He proposes distinguishing violent acts of destruction/annihilation, including internal phenomena such as the annihilation of thought, from the seductive lure into a world of non-thinking, Freud's pleasant "Nirvana-like" state, or the silent pull towards a state of mind that comes close to the absence of tension. The third manifestation of the death drive corresponds to the sadistic control of objects that prevents movement yet is associated with a peculiar pleasure. This third perspective considers destructiveness as a more continuous quality, in the framework of which superiority is asserted by finding faults in everything, thereby leading to a triumph of ignorance over knowledge. In this case, the aim is not annihilation per se but rather the maintenance of a kind of paralysis: the object is kept half alive so that it can be treated sadistically. Common to all three models is the importance ascribed to attacks on thinking. Nevertheless, uncertainty remains: is this hatred of thought a kind of irreducible datum or a manifestation of a deeper process? There are recurring questions: How could such diverse manifestations of the death drive be assembled into a metapsychological concept that explains the deepest source of human motivation? How is the concept of the death drive rooted in biology, and how does this impact its psychological representation and understanding? Finally, how does the concept of the death drive contribute to the question of what causes aggression?

Bipolarity of the drives was central to Freud's understanding of the psyche (Freud, 1937, p. 243). The Kleinian tradition took this bipolarity up but separated the concept of the drive from its biological counterpart in Freud's initial presentation, describing its functioning in purely psychological terms (Bell, 2015). Klein emphasized that she did not employ the life and death instincts as general behavioural concepts of the biological organism but rather as mental phenomena underpinning love and hate. She argued that human infants struggle with impulses of love and hate as well as with experiences of fragmentation and anxiety from birth onwards; and that primary anxiety emerges in conjunction with the fear of being annihilated by a destructive force within that is associated to the ego "falling to pieces." This breakdown of the mind was regarded as a consequence of the destructive force and a defence against it, but also as one of its forms of expression. One should note that for Klein the collapse of the mind is death, not a watered-down, limited version of it (Blass, 2014, p. 95). One's mind is felt to be no longer there or no longer able to think. Melanie Klein developed her very concrete, vivid language of part objects and bodily functions through work with small children. Extrapolating backwards, she assumed that infants felt and thought in the same way, and, further, that this is the language of thinking and feeling in everyone's unconscious (Spillius, 1983). Klein attempted to put into words per-verbal experiences by describing the ways bodily and sensory experiences are registered in the mind. To have a phantasy of a devouring object is not only to feel incorporated into another; it also means experiencing the death of the mind – or, more precisely, the death of part of the mind. These unconscious phantasies are both inherent and generated from experience. They shape the infant's reality; and infants employ the mental mechanisms of projection and introjection to manage their experience and psychic survival.

Klein's descriptions of the fate of life and death instincts cannot be understood without the concept of an inner world inhabited by objects that are important for the development of the self. For Melanie Klein, relatedness with human content was always at the very core of human existence. The destruction arising from within (the death drive) is deflected outwards, thus creating a persecutory world; the baby that hates imagines a hateful breast, which he or she then internalizes, thus creating the psychological foundation of violent attacks upon self and object. Thus, the destroyed object, which is the inherent expression of the person's destructive impulses, is regarded as a destroyed part of the self. The internalized anti-life breast is also the prototype of an envious internal relationship and becomes the heir of the death drive within.

Even though Klein talks of annihilation of objects, these are never actually destroyed. Rather, we are here dealing with an infinite dialectic of destruction that can never end, as every object that is attacked re-emerges as a persecutor.

These processes cannot be understood psychoanalytically without postulating an object on the recipient side of projections and destructiveness that is, hopefully, able to act as counter force, namely a mother, who perceives and helps the baby in this struggle. Melanie Klein's thinking was not created ex nihilo. Although it is very difficult to figure out who influenced whom, it would be interesting to take into account that Ferenczi's (1929) essay "The Unwelcome Child and the Death Instinct" was one of the first to make use of the concept from an object relational perspective (Bergmann, 2011). Ferenczi proposed that the human baby is not born with a strong wish to live; it must be welcomed into the world with love and coaxed into finding life worth living. When the child is not welcomed it will prefer not to fight for its survival and at times even turn inward and die. The importance of the developmental factor was put into focus by Rosenfeld (1987) and De Masi. Hanna Segal, too, recognized the importance of constitutional factors. However, she repeatedly stressed how the nature of the environment, in particular the real care offered by the mother, crucially affects the process. The rejection of dependency and the development of pathological structures depend mostly on an unfortunate or traumatic emotional relationship with the caregivers. A persistent lack of maternal empathy may be traumatic (Steiner, 2015).

What all these descriptions lack is an explanation on the interaction or the interplay between psyche and soma, therefore they cannot be easily reconciled with the idea of an instinctual definition as a psychical representation of organic vectors. This is further complicated by the fact that Freud used the term "instinct" in two distinct ways: first, to delineate a psychic representation in the framework of a dualistic conception, and second, as a metaphysical law governing biological substance. This dual usage has aggravated the difficulties with regard to the general determination of conceptual content and the creation of a reliable concept topography.

A prominent effort to integrate these various conceptual approaches was undertaken by Kernberg in various publications (2001, 2009). Kernberg proposes treating affects as the primary motivations of behaviour. Affects include a fundamental communicative function in the infant/

caregiver relationship. The integration of positive and negative affects in the framework of this relationship makes possible the crystallization of libido and aggression as superordinate motivational systems or drives. The drives manifest themselves by activating their constituent affects with varying intensity, along the line of libidinal and aggressive invest-ments. In other words, affects as primary motivators are organized into hierarchically supra-ordinate motivations corresponding to the Freud-ian drives. The latter, in turn, become activated in the form of their affectively valenced components. Representations manifest themselves as unconscious phantasies. Just as erotic desire "leans on" the biological apparatus of sexual excitement, hatred "leans on" the primary affect of rage. Both affects are aroused or emerge for the first time in the context of the earliest object relations. Rage is one of the fundamental affects, an inborn biological response that acquires its function as the originator of hatred only in the context of the internalization of persecutory, "all bad," internalized object relations. The affect of hatred, a complex and central aspect of the death drive, involves in its most primitive form not only the desire to destroy the object but also to destroy the awareness of the relationship with it. According to Kernberg, the concept of the death drive as a designation for the dominant unconscious motivation toward self-destructiveness should be warranted to severe cases of psychopa-thology. He questions whether severe self-destructive aggression is a primary tendency and proposes as an alternative that the unconscious function of self-destructiveness is not simply to destroy the self but to destroy significant others as well.

Claudia Frank (2015) suggests another way of solving the dilemma surrounding the use of the term "death drive." She suggests it might be appropriate to consider Melanie Klein's concept of an evil principle – along with the pleasure and reality principles – as less ambiguous than the use of the awkward term of the death drive concept that fostered and fosters misunderstanding due to its philosophical dimensions and biological metaphors. She argues that what Freud clinically intended in 1920 was to develop a concept to describe self-destructive clinical phenomena. This was his primary purpose of accounting for the forces beyond the pleasure principle. Accordingly, the extensive denial or disregard of the death drive concept in German-speaking regions after 1945 might be understood as an expression of and defence against an "evil principle." Confronting its implications represents an unending task and only appears conceivable if there is also an idea in the mind of reparation, a concept that Melanie Klein developed in the 1920s, like-wise on the basis of her analyses of young children.

Conclusion

The concept of the death drive remains a useful lens for describing destructive clinical processes whose compulsive libidinous destructive quality should not be overlooked. Theoretically, it remains a difficult concept.

Perhaps we can tolerate the structural fuzziness better when we accept that psychoanalysis does not offer a closed set of well-organized theories but a set of models that help us handle the heterogeneous emergent psychic realities. These models or theories are available for multiple applications and stimulate the formulation of further questions. These open concepts provide an active and flexible access to an autopoietic reality of the psyche. They can be used to address the difference between singularities as well as the distance between general logic and empirical reality (Schülein, 2003). Like in the case of Oedipus complex, we must describe in detail what we are talking about in each single case. It may even be preferable to keep multiple paradigms and perspectives with regard to the death drive as a primary form of experience and as a metapsychological term. As aggression is rooted in biology, why should we give up the term "drive," which comes so close to the quality of the experiences in the struggle between the two principles? When a patient retreats over the weekend in a state of mindlessness and ends up devaluing all help that is offered, having the concept of death drive in mind ensures that we do not play down the destructive forces he or she is fighting with. By contrast, it is a risk to reify the concept, relying on it as an all-embracing formula. This could give way to short-cuts. Instead of all too simple explanations, we need careful and precise descriptions and interpretations. These descriptions should include both the destructive and the dependent/libidinal self as containing both good and bad aspects and explain the processes that bring about and maintain this complex arrangement. What is the relation between internal objects and parts of the self? How is it that a bad internal object is sometimes, and in some patients, felt to be a separate entity inside the personality, whereas at other times, and in other patients, it takes over the ego in a destructive amalgam? With this in mind, it appears that the death drive is not a causal explanation for anything but rather a set of tools that are useful for exploring the complexity of destructiveness.

Note

1   Herbert Rosenfeld, born in Germany in 1910, emigrated to England in 1935 and underwent analysis with Melanie Klein. His seminal paper "A Clinical Approach to the Psychoanalytic Theory of the Life and Death Instincts: An Investigation Into the Aggressive Aspects of Narcissism" was an invited contribution to the 27th International Psychoanalytical Congress, Vienna, 1971. For the Vienna Psychoanalytic Society this was a very remarkable event: for the first time after the war Anna Freud returned to Vienna to open the Sigmund Freud Museum in Berggasse. At that time, there were only sporadic publications in German about the clinical application of the death drive. The majority of these were translations, mainly from English, of works by analysts who had emigrated from Germany (Frank, 2015).

References

Bell, D. (2015). The death drive: Phenomenological perspectives in contemporary Kleinian theory. *International Journal of Psychoanalysis, 96*:411–423.

Bergmann, M. S. (2011). The dual impact of Freud's death and Freud's death instinct theory on the history of psychoanalysis. *Psychoanalytical Review, 98*:665–686.

Blass, R. B. (2014). On "the fear of death" as the primary anxiety: How and why Klein differs from Freud. *International Journal of Psychoanalysis, 95*:613–627.

De Masi, F. (2015). Is the concept of the death drive still useful in the clinical field? *International Journal of Psychoanalysis, 96*:445–458.

Feldman, M. (2000). Views on the manifestation of the death instinct in clinical work. *International Journal of Psychoanalysis, 81*:53–65.

Fenichel, O. (1938). The drive to amass wealth. *Psychoanalytic Quarterly, 7*:69–95.

Ferenczi, S. (1929). The unwelcome child and the death instinct. *International Journal of Psychoanalysis, 10*:125–129.

Frank, C. (2009). *Melanie Klein in Berlin: Her First Psychoanalyses of Children.* London: Routledge.

Frank, C. (2011). Zum Ringen mit Manifestationen des Todestriebs: Theoretische und klinische Aspekte. *Jahrbuch der Psychoanalyse, 62*:75–96.

Frank, C. (2015). On the reception of the concept of the death drive in Germany: Expressing and resisting an "evil principle"? *International Journal of Psychoanalysis*, 96:425–444.

Frank, C., & Weiss, H. (1996). The origins of disquieting discoveries by Melanie Klein: The possible significance of the case of "Erna". *International Journal of Psychoanalysis*, 77:1101–1126.

Freud, S. (1914). *On Narcissism: An Introduction*. Standard Edition 14:67–102.

Freud, S. (1920). *Beyond the Pleasure Principle*. Standard Edition 18:1–64.

Freud, S. (1923). *The Ego and the Id*. Standard Edition 19:1–66.

Freud, S. (1924). *The Economic Problem of Masochism*. Standard Edition 19:155–170.

Freud, S. (1930). *Civilization and Its Discontents*. Standard Edition 21:57–146.

Freud, S. (1937). *Analysis Terminable and Interminable*. Standard Edition 23:209–254.

Jekels, L., & Bergler, E. (1940). Instinct dualism in Dreams. *Psychoanalytic Quarterly*, 9:394–414.

Jones, E. (1957). *Sigmund Freud Life and Work (Volume Three: The Last Phase 1919–1939)*. London: The Hogarth Press.

Kernberg, O. F. (2001). Object relations, affects, and drives. *Psychoanalytic Inquiry*, 21:604–619.

Kernberg, O. F. (2009). The concept of the death drive: A clinical perspective. *International Journal of Psychoanalysis*, 90:1009–1023.

King, P., & Steiner, R. (1991). *The Freud–Klein Controversies 1941–45*. London: Tavistock.

Klein, M. (1932). *The Psycho-Analysis of Children*. London: The Hogarth Press.

Klein, M. (1935). A contribution to the psychogenesis of manic-depressive states. *International Journal of Psychoanalysis*, 16:145–174.

Klein, M. (1946). Notes on some schizoid mechanisms. *International Journal of Psychoanalysis*, 27:99–110.

Klein, M. (1958). On the development of mental functioning. In: *Envy and Gratitude and Other Works 1946–1963* (pp. 236–246). London: The Hogarth Press.

Klein, M. (1975). Explanatory notes. In: *Envy and Gratitude and Other Works 1946–1963* (pp. 324–336). London: The Hogarth Press.

Lampl-De Groot, J. (1933). Problems of femininity. *Psychoanalytic Quarterly*, 2:489–518.

Laub, D., & Lee, S. (2003). Thanatos and massive psychic trauma. *Journal of American Psychoanalytic Association*, 51:433–463.

Loewald, H. W. (1972). Freud's conception of the negative therapeutic reaction with comments on instinct theory. *Journal of American Psychoanalytic Association*, 20:235–245.

Meltzer, D. (1968). Terror, persecution, dread: A dissection of paranoid anxieties. *International Journal of Psychoanalysis*, *49*:396–400.

Rosenfeld, H. (1971). A clinical approach to the psychoanalytic theory of the life and death instincts: An investigation into the aggressive aspects of narcissism. *International Journal of Psychoanalysis*, *52*:169–178.

Rosenfeld, H. (1987). *Impasse and interpretation* new library of psychoanalysis. London and New York: Tavistock Publications and the Institute of Psycho-Analysis, 1.

Schülein, J. A. (2003). On the logic of psychoanalytic theory. *International Journal of Psychoanalysis*, *84*:315–330.

Segal, H. (1993). On the clinical usefulness of the concept of death instinct. *International Journal of Psychoanalysis*, *74*:55–61.

Spillius, E. B. (1983). Some developments from the work of Melanie Klein. *International Journal of Psychoanalysis*, *64*:321–332.

Spillius, E. B., Milton, J., Garvey, P., Couve, C., & Steiner, D. (2011). *The New Dictionary of Kleinian Thought*. London: Routledge.

Steiner, J. (2015). Reflections on the work of Hanna Segal (1918–2011). *International Journal of Psychoanalysis*, *96*:165–175.

Stevens, K. (1930). Pain, love and fear. *Psychoanalytic Review*, *17*:126–139.

CHAPTER 2

Laplanche as a reader of "Beyond the Pleasure Principle"

Friedl Früh
Translated by Sam Simon

This is a chapter about Laplanche's way of reading Freud's text "Beyond the Pleasure Principle," as recorded in his book *Life & Death in Psychoanalysis* (Laplanche, 1970).

Recently, Ulrike May (2013) from Berlin published a truly well-researched and meticulously crafted paper that places Freud's introduction of the concept of the death drive in the context of his earlier theoretical works. I would recommend studying May's article to anyone interested in the development of Freud's ideas. May's research shows that the paper published by Freud in 1920, "Beyond the Pleasure Principle" (Freud, 1920), was preceded by an original version from the year 1919, the same year "A Child Is Being Beaten" (Freud, 1919) was published. This earlier version differs considerably from the published one. In the context of the present volume, it will not be possible to thoroughly discuss this issue. However, with regard to my discussion of Laplanche's ideas, it is important to highlight that already in 1919, the year "A Child Is Being Beaten" was published, there existed, as shown by Ulrike May's research, a first draft of "Beyond the Pleasure Principle," that substantially differs from the final version from 1920, and that Jean Laplanche had in his theories already referred to the ideas from "A Child Is Being Beaten," at a time when he presumably did not yet know that Freud's first version of "Beyond the Pleasure Principle" was elaborated in the same year that "A Child Is Being Beaten" was published. It is important to emphasize this point because Laplanche also holds that fundamental deliberations in "Beyond the Pleasure Principle" were first formulated in "A Child Is Being Beaten." Furthermore, this example reveals a way of examination of Freud's theoretical and clinical concepts that is characteristic for Laplanche. He, like almost no other expert of Freud's work, has observed the evolution of Freudian theory from its very beginnings, giving it due reference in his own "General Seduction Theory." In my view, this holds especially true for Laplanche's understanding of "Beyond the Pleasure Principle."

In *Life & Death in Psychoanalysis*, Laplanche calls Freud's text "Beyond the Pleasure Principle" "the most fascinating and baffling text of the entire Freudian *corpus*" (Laplanche, 1970, p. 106). He makes connections to all the periods of Freud's works. He begins with the "Project for a Scientific Psychology" (Freud, 1950 [1895]), where the economic issue is the main topic. In the "Three Essays on the Theory of Sexuality" (Freud, 1905), the focus is on infantile sexuality. "Instincts and Their Vicissitudes" (Freud, 1915) describes the drive turning from an active mode into a passive one. Freud's essay "On Narcissism: An Introduction" (1914) deals with love for the ego as a whole object. Finally and most notably, "A Child Is Being Beaten" (1919) is about sexual masochism. The problem of masochism was again addressed in a paper written after the publication of "Beyond the Pleasure Principle" (cf. Freud, 1924).

Laplanche presented his theory of a *Sexual Death Drive* at an international forum at the EPA congress in Marseille in 1984. His presentation instigated an international debate on his reading of "Beyond the Pleasure Principle." Laplanche disagreed with many interpreters of Freud's work, for instance, Ernest Jones, who thought that the introduction of the death drive in Freudian psychoanalysis was a reaction to the death of Freud's daughter Sophie. Nor did Laplanche see the introduction of the death drive by Freud as a total disruption or discontinuity, or even as a fundamental change with respect to his preceding theories. For Laplanche, the introduction of the death drive was a necessity born from the evolution of theoretical construction itself, especially following the introduction of the concept of narcissism in "On Narcissism: An Introduction" in 1914. In this essay, Freud advocated a close association between the amplified libidinal cathexis of the ego and the binding function of the ego. This, in turn, necessitated the establishment of the death drive as an antagonist to account for the resolving, parturient, destructive forces of psychic life.

On the subject of "Beyond the Pleasure Principle," Laplanche writes: "Never had Freud shown himself to be as profoundly *free* and audacious as in that vast metapsychological, metaphysical and metabiological fresco" (1970, p. 106). He went on to argue that the reason the text was so profoundly baffling had to do with the fact that Freud's discourse is only sporadically and superficially subordinated to logical imperatives:

> it constitutes a mode of thought that is free (in the sense of free associations), is undertaken "in order to see," and implies a series of "about-faces," acts of virtual repentance, and denials. *That* (equally attractive) counterpart of the freedom of Freud's style of inquiry may well disappoint the reader, who fails to identify with that style: the holes in the reasoning constitute so many traps; the sliding of concepts results in blurring terminological points of reference; the most far reaching discussions are suddenly resolved in the most arbitrary manner. [. . .] *Seductive and traumatic* as this was, the forced introduction of the death drive could only provoke every conceivable variety of defense on the part of Freud's heirs: a deliberate refusal on the part of some; a purely scholastic acceptance of the notion and of the dualism Eros-Thanatos on the part of others; a qualified acceptance, cutting off from its philosophical bases, by an author like Melanie Klein; and most frequently of all, a passing allusion or a total forgetting of the notion.
>
> (Laplanche, 1970, p. 107)

It seems to me that Laplanche, with his incorruptible way of thinking, has managed to uphold a very necessary disposition with regard to the passionately illogical text of "Beyond the Pleasure Principle," this bursting-at-the-seams oeuvre. To understand the spirit of free association requires taking it seriously in a genuine analytical sense. Claiming something he steadfastly demanded as homage to the great thinker, Laplanche insisted that, after Freud, one had to allow his thoughts to continue to work, letting them continually develop in order to evolve their great potential. Laplanche called this *"faire travailler Freud."*

To understand what I am referring to, I would like to stress once more how many of Freud's original ideas – deliberations on the subject of drive energy (the operating life's economical aspect) in the *Project*, the development of an understanding of sexually determined sadomasochism in the "Three Essays on Sexuality" or in the paper "A Child Is Being Beaten" – were further developed and complemented with new aspects in subsequent works. This is the case of the reversal of active and passive drive destiny in "Instincts and Their Vicissitudes," *whereby* the reflexive form of turning-back onto the own self made it possible to restructure the role of phantasy. In a similar vein, the introduction of the concept of narcissism in 1914 had implications with respect to the explanation of destructiveness. Through the introduction of the death drive, earlier ideas were given a new form. Nonetheless, it is probably also true that Freud accomplished all this at the cost of clarity, ending up writing an extremely confusing document.

In *The So-Called "Death Drive": A Sexual Drive* (Laplanche, 2004), Laplanche stated the key premises for understanding the death drive as follows:

1   The supposed original conflict between life and death drives is absolutely not a biological opposition which exists in the living being, and consequently it has no pertinence to the science of biology.
2   This opposition is uniquely and wholly located in the domain of the human being – and not as a difference between sexuality and a non-sexual aggression, but in the heart of sexuality itself. If the Freudian terminology is to be retained, one should insert the adjective "sexual," talking of the *sexual death drives* versus the *sexual life* drives.
3   Rather than two hypothetical biological forces, this opposition concerns two distinct mechanisms in the sphere of human fantasy: the bound (secondary) process and the unbound (primary) process. Or, more accurately, two principles: the principle of binding, which would introduce order from the sexual life drives, and the principle of unbinding, which takes its power from the sexual death drives.

(p. 455)

In Laplanche's understanding, this thesis-like summary goes to the heart of the intrinsic contradiction that runs like a common thread through the entirety of "Beyond the Pleasure Principle": the discrepancy between a so-called biological reality and the psychoanalytically relevant principle of the mind's psychic processes. In Laplanche's view, the contradiction between a concrete conception of reality and a theory of human psychic reality was already established with Freud's dismissal of the seduction theory in 1897. This is the basis of Laplanche's own "General Seduction Theory" (Laplanche, 1987). It is beyond the scope of the present chapter to discuss this work. However, I do think that the very same issues in that book are also tackled, albeit on a different level, through the notion of, as Laplanche calls it, a "sexual death drive."

In brief, Laplanche's argument in his "General Seduction Theory" is as follows: Freud's abandonment of the seduction theory in September 1897 in the famous letter to Fließ (Masson, 1985, pp. 259–260) marks a "going astray." The relationship infant-adult is from the beginning marked by compromised messages that come from the adult's unconscious handling of the baby in the care-taking situation. Those messages cannot be understood by the infant because of its lack of an understanding of adult sexuality. Still these messages constitute the basis for an ongoing process of translation within the human being itself. The "General Seduction Theory" concentrates on the situation established between baby and adult. Insofar as the baby is from the beginning of his or her life dependent on the adult to survive, this relationship is from the baby's perspective determined by the genuine equivalence between dependency and passivity.

Laplanche, in his interpretation of Freud's letter to Fließ, loves to cite the very end of that letter, which is often forgotten: "I have to add one more thing. In this collapse of everything valuable, the psychological alone has remained untouched. The dream [book] stands entirely secure and my beginnings of the metapsychological work have only grown in my estimation. It is a pity that one cannot make a living, for instance, on dream interpretation!" (Masson, 1985, p. 266). This saying is obviously in complete contradiction to the earlier proclaimed reasons for the abandonment of the seduction theory.

Before Laplanche approached the introduction of a death drive in his book *Life & Death in Psychoanalysis*, he explained Freud's important distinction between aggression and sadism in the chapter titled "Aggressiveness and Sadomasochism" (Laplanche, 1970, pp. 85–102). According to Laplanche, aggression belongs to the realm of self-preservation, sadism to that of sexuality. Laplanche picks up on Freud's ideas from "Instincts and Their Vicissitudes" – notably the reflexive shift from active to passive in the form of a turning on oneself, an idea that is presented here for the first time – and refers mainly to "A Child Is Being Beaten." In the latter paper, Freud treats the nature of masochism as something rooted in the unconscious. The wish – "my father beats me" – can only be interpreted as a surrogate for the wish to be sexually seduced by the father. This wish cannot be made conscious. It rather remains a construction of analysis. Its efficacy is proven by the fact that the wish is accompanied by sexual excitation, which is released through a masturbatory act. I regret deeply that I will only be able to depict the Laplanchean method of understanding in brief sketches. A more thorough analysis requires an intimate knowledge of more than just the two Freud papers mentioned earlier. In any case, a key point is that in Laplanche's conception, the concept of aggression differs fundamentally from the concept of masochism. Therefore, the concept of destruction that is introduced in "Beyond the Pleasure Principle" and is termed aggression there for the first time, has to be seen first and foremost as a form of self-destruction – a turning around on oneself. This is an essential presupposition for the introduction of a "Sexual Death Drive" as proposed by Laplanche. For Laplanche, an understanding of the death drive as "pure, non-sexual aggressivity," as advocated, for instance, by Paula Heimann in her Kleinian period (cf. Heimann, 1952), is obsolete. Laplanche writes that, "in her article 'Notes on the theory of the life and death instincts' [Heimann, 1952] she claims that what brought the death drive to the fore was the experience of a destructiveness of a chemical purity, so to speak, which is only termed sexual falsely" (2004, p. 459). Laplanche's laconical comment on this statement by Paula Heimann simply is:

> The Kleinian reversal is remarkable here, for it is pushed to the limit. With Freud, one should insist to the present day on the fact that people refuse to acknowledge what is sexual in their behaviour; here, on the contrary, sexuality is nothing but a false alibi to allow the release of pure aggression!
>
> (2004, p. 459)

Another relevant dimension that is recognized and taken up by Laplanche is the economic aspect:

> From an economic point of view the major contradiction consists in attributing to a single "drive" the tendency towards the radical elimination of all tension, the supreme form of the pleasure principle, and the masochistic search for unpleasure, which in all logic, can only be interpreted as an increase of tension.
>
> (Laplanche, 1970, p. 108)

The stringent necessity for Freud to introduce the concept of a death drive in 1919/1920 is seen by Laplanche as most apparent in Freud's 1914 treatise "On Narcissism: An Introduction." In this work Freud broadens the scope of his theoretical construct through the idea of a libidinous occupation of not just another person but of the ego itself as an agent of attachment instead of detachment, signifying the effect of the secondary process in contrast to the effect of the primary process. Said ego now accumulates all the power; it transforms this into the Eros that serves to tame the erotic excitement and can help to transfer it into a connection with the tender tendencies (also stemming from the relationships with the parents). Under the Eros' weight, the infantile sexual, an entity that Freud initially called "presexual-sexual," appears to forfeit its importance. In the context of the death drive, however, which Laplanche termed the "sexual death drive," infantile sexuality, the auto-erotic, the untethered, all celebrate a rebirth:

> The energy of the sexual drive, as is known, was called 'libido.' Born of a formalistic concern for symmetry, the term "destrudo" once proposed to designate the energy of the death drive, did not survive a single day. For the Death Drive does not possess its own energy. Its energy is libido. Or, better put, the Death Drive is the very soul, the constitutive principle, of libidinal circulation.
>
> (Laplanche, 1970, p. 124)

There is simply no other force than this libido that endures and sustains all the fates and fortunes of life and love. Even the concept of repetition compulsion – likewise newly positioned (constructed) in "Beyond the Pleasure Principle" and named a loyal servant to the death drive – shows its true face as a constructive principle of analytical work from the very beginnings of the treatment. How else than through the process of repetition could the individual psychic mechanisms between wishful phantasies and fear of destruction be revealed – on occasion through or from the failure of the process or even because of it.

If we place the terms constituting the constant pairs of opposites in Freud's thinking face to face, the genealogy takes a strange form:

- Primary process – free energy – unbinding – sexuality becomes Eros;
- Secondary process – bound energy – binding – ego – becomes death drive.

As Laplanche puts it:

> Opposite the ego, a binding, vital form, the *death drive* is the last theo-
> retical instance serving to designate a logos that would necessarily be
> mute. . . . Absent from every unconscious, death is perhaps rediscovered
> in the unconscious as the most radical, but also most sterile, principle of
> its logic. But it is life which crystallizes the first objects to which desire
> attaches itself, before even thought can cling to them.
>
> (1970, p. 126)

Sexuality in its significance of a sexual unconscious is recognizable clearer with Laplanche than with many of Freud's successors, particularly in the concept of a sexual death drive that Laplanche sees to be at work in "Beyond the Pleasure Principle." In Freud's succession it was sexuality that was sacrificed on the altar of the Eros, oftentimes invoking "Beyond the Pleasure Principle." This sacrificial offering was made willingly within parts of the psychoanalytic community.

References

Freud, S. (1905). *Three Essays on the Theory of Sexuality*. Standard Edition 7:123–246.

Freud, S. (1914). *On Narcissism: An Introduction*. Standard Edition 14:67–102.

Freud, S. (1915). *Instincts and Their Vicissitudes*. Standard Edition 14:109–140.

Freud, S. (1919). *A Child Is Being Beaten*. Standard Edition 17:185–204.

Freud, S. (1920). *Beyond the Pleasure Principle*. Standard Edition 18:1–64.

Freud, S. (1924). *The Economic Problem of Masochism*. Standard Edition 19:155–170.

Freud, S. (1950 [1895]). *Project for a Scientific Psychology*. Standard Edition 1:281–391.

Heimann, P. (1952). Notes on the theory of the life and death instincts. In: M. Klein, P. Heimann, S. Isaacs & J. Riviere (Eds.), *Developments in Psychoanalysis* (pp. 321–337). London: Karnac, 1989.

Laplanche, J. (1985 [1970]). *Life & Death in Psychoanalysis*. Baltimore: The Johns Hopkins University Press.

Laplanche, J. (1989 [1987]). *New Foundations for Psychoanalysis*. Oxford: Basil Blackwell.

Laplanche, J. (2004). The so-called "death drive": A sexual drive. *British Journal of Psychotherapy*, 20:455–471.

Masson, J. M. (1985). *The Complete Letters of Sigmund Freud to Wilhelm Fliess 1887–1904*. Cambridge: Harvard University Press.

May, U. (2015 [2013]). The third step in drive theory: On the genesis of "Beyond the Pleasure Principle". *Psychoanalytic History*, 17:205–272.

CHAPTER 3

Unexpected antecedents to the concept of the death drive: a return to the beginnings

Jeanne Wolff Bernstein

Near the end of his life, Freud had to admit to himself and his readers that

> I am well aware that the dualistic theory according to which an instinct
> of death or of destruction or aggression claims equal rights as a partner
> with Eros as manifested in the libido, has found little sympathy and has
> not really been accepted even among analysts.
>
> (1937, p. 244)

Feeling abandoned and misunderstood by the majority of his fellow
analysts and friends who found little to admire in the concept of a life
and death drive, Freud was all the more elated to find a fellow thinker/
philosopher in the figure of the Greek philosopher, Empedocles of
Acragas (born about 495 B.C.) who also

> taught that two principles governed events in the life of the universe
> and in the life of the mind, and that those principles were everlastingly
> at war with each other. He called them (φιλία) love and (νεῖκος) strife.
> Of these two powers – which he conceived of as being 'at bottom natu-
> ral forces operating like instincts, and by no means intelligences with a
> conscious purpose' – the one strives to agglomerate the primal particles

of the four elements into a single unity, while the other, on the contrary, seeks to undo all those fusions and to separate the primal particles of the elements from one another. Empedocles thought of the process of the universe as a continuous, never-ceasing alternation of periods.

(1937, p. 246)

Freud was very pleased to find so much alikeness between the great Greek philosopher[1] and his last elaboration of the death instinct, which he asserts in 1937,

> are both in name and function, the same as our two primal instincts, *Eros and destructiveness, the first of which endeavors to combine what exists into ever greater unities, while the second endeavors to dissolve those combinations and to destroy the structures to which they have given rise.*

(1937, p. 246, italics added)

In "Analysis Terminable and Interminable" (1937), one of his last clinical texts, Freud writes that the search for pleasure (*Lustprinzip*) was no longer sufficient to explain phenomena like the negative therapeutic reaction, masochism, and an unconscious sense of guilt, but that another force, Freud calls it "power," existed to explain these essentially self-attacking/self-destructive phenomena. Here I quote Freud again:

> These phenomena are unmistakable indications of a presence of a power in mental life which we call the instinct of aggression or of destruction according to its aims, and which we trace back to the original death instinct of living matter. It is not a question of an antithesis between an optimistic and a pessimistic theory of life.

(1937, p. 243)

Rather, and here Freud becomes very foreboding,

> only by the concurrent or mutually opposing action of the two primal instincts – Eros and the death instinct, never by one or the other alone, can we explain the rich multiplicity of the phenomena of life.

(1937, p. 243)

Even though Freud officially introduced Eros and Thanatos as late as 1920, there were many precursors to his theory in his earlier writings; precursors which are not ordinarily associated with the death drive. According to Freud, Eros seeks union with another object, is thus object-oriented and more differentiated than the death drive, which seeks a state of "no-tension." Eros is there to bind, to establish greater unities, and being a descendant of Freud's earlier sexual drive, it safeguards life and vitality. Eros works towards the prolongation of life and is turned towards the love object. The death drive, on the other hand, seeks a state of no-tension (Nirvana) and searches for the dissolution and destruction of vital unities. This eviscerating force strives towards a state of complete repose and towards the restoration of inanimate matter.

As will become clear later, the forerunner of Freud's death drive was his earlier self-preservative drive, which was egoistic and narcissistic in nature and was directed inwards towards the preservation of one's own self. So, paradoxically, this self-preservative drive, which would later become the death drive was already libidinally invested, foreshadowing in a curious way the much later fusion of both the life and death drive which Lacan would eventually articulate with his concept of *jouissance*. The idea of going back, of restoring, implying a tendency of the psyche to reduce all tension, has had a long history in psychoanalysis. Already in "The Project for a Scientific Psychology" (1950) Freud writes that "the mind aims at a reduction of excitation and longs for a state of inertia." He also writes, "We have a certain knowledge of a trend in psychical life towards avoiding unpleasure, we are tempted to identify that trend with the primary trend towards inertia" (1950, p. 297). In "The Interpretation of Dreams" (1900), on the other hand, both the idea of "returning to daemonic forces at night" (p. 614) and the dream's capacity of "reaching back into our past heritage," underscore the conservative and regressive nature of the yet to be developed death drive. Freud writes,

> The fact that dreams are hypermnesic and have access to material from childhood has become one of the cornerstones of our teaching. Our theory regards wishes originating in infancy as the indispensable motive force for the formation of dreams.
>
> (1900, p. 591)

We thus see in these early texts of "The Project" and "The Interpretation of Dreams" that the idea of preservation and conservation, going back to a primitive state of affairs *and of a drive that goes back to a primary process thinking*, is part and parcel of Freud's early thinking, foreshadowing the death drive. In "The Three Essays on Sexuality" (1905), Freud introduces a new perspective, by privileging the drive over the object; he argues that there is an initial stage of auto-eroticism, a drive that is not directed towards other objects but to the infant's own body as a pleasurable zone. In this same text, he also mentions for the first time the idea of self-preservation, an antecedent of the later death drive and he puts forth the idea that sexual activity (the later Eros) attaches itself to functions of self-preservation and becomes independent of it later. In other words, Freud essentially argues here that infantile sexuality is auto-erotic and that the sexual drive is made up of components that are disconnected and independent of one another, purely searching for pleasure. The discovery of an external object which gives pleasure and unites is a late discovery. In other words, the strive to live, to connect, to bind, to unite – all characteristics of the later Eros, is a later development than the self-preservative one, which needs to watch out for survival and experiences the urgency of conserving and of reclining upon itself.

These self-preservative forces take on a more libidinized nature in Freud's mind over time and become more closely associated with the death drive.

In a little known and read paper, "The Psychogenic Disturbance of Vision" (1910), Freud finally introduces by name the two opposing drives: the drive for self-preservation and the sexual drive. He states that they are not compatible and come into conflict with one another. He writes,

> We have discovered that every instinct tries to make itself effective by activating ideas that are in keeping with its aims. These instincts are not compatible with one another; their interests come into conflict. . . . From that point of view our attempted explanation, an especially important part is played by the undeniable opposition between the instincts which subserve sexuality, the attainment of sexual pleasure, and those other instincts, which have as their own aim the self-preservation of the individual, the ego instincts.
>
> (1910, pp. 213–214)

But it is only in his groundbreaking paper "On Narcissism" (1914) that Freud expands upon the idea of the self-preservative and object-related drives; the self-preservative drives become the narcissistic drives, which include such prosaic states as dreaming, sleeping, being sick, and primary process thinking, in other words, states where we go back and restore our vital functions, thereby shielding us from the outside expediencies of life (*Nöte des Lebens*). In opposition to these narcissistic drives, Freud sets the object-related/sexual drives, where the ego sends out cathexes to the outside object, as happens in the case of being in love, where the subject gives all his libidinal investments to the object and the ego becomes impoverished, while in the case of sickness, the libidinal investments are all withdrawn upon the ego and the subject is exclusively preoccupied with himself. Freud famously states in "On Narcissism," that

> the individual actually carries on a double existence, one designed to serve his own purposes (ego drive/later death drive) and another as a link in a chain in which he serves against any volition of his own sexual/ life drive. In the last resort we must begin to love in order not to fall ill and we fall ill if we never let ourselves be loved.
>
> (1914, p. 85)

One year later, in 1915, but only published in 1917, Freud conceives of a new structure, apart from the hysterical and obsessional structure: and develops, after his long studies with the Bürghölzli/Swiss school, the structure of melancholia (Freud, 1917). In melancholia the subject, in an identification with the lost object, becomes the lost object, and folds/falls back upon himself, ensconcing himself in a state of extreme narcissism that is directed toward his own self-destruction and auto-distinction. The other has no access to him because the melancholic, being closely related in his pathography to the psychotic, is fundamentally so involved with his own suffering that he foregoes and abandons the links to the outside world, and in so doing, even risks his own death. There is one more text that precedes "Beyond the Pleasure Principle" that is of importance for my argument: Freud's text on "The Uncanny" (1919), in which Freud resurrects the idea of the daemonic force which he had already described in "The Interpretation of Dreams," but now he links it more clearly and powerfully with the idea of the repetition compulsion, which will gain more prominence a year later in "Beyond the Pleasure Principle." He writes in 1919,

> for it is possible to recognize the dominance in the unconscious mind of a compulsion to repeat proceeding from the instinctual impulses and probably inherent in the very nature of the instincts, a compulsion powerful enough to overrule the pleasure principle, lending to certain aspects of the mind, their *daemonic* character. . . . Whatever is perceived as a compulsion to repeat is perceived as uncanny.
>
> (p. 238)

What is it precisely that is repeated, so as to produce an uncanny effect? The answer Freud gives is: all the magical, omnipotent beliefs we cling to in states of helplessness and that we do not want to give up. What appears to us as being uncanny are the omnipotent wishes/phantasies we do not want to abandon. However, if we hold onto these narcissistic wishes for too long and mis-take our wishes/phantasies for reality, we play once again with the possibility of our own self-destruction. We risk mistaking our uncanny wishes for a constant, ongoing smile, like that of the doll Olympia in "The Sandman Story," for something real.

In "Beyond The Pleasure Principle" (1920), Freud finally arrives at the grand introduction of Eros and the death drive. He explains his own development in the following way:

> We came to know what the sexual drives were from their relation to the sexes and to the reproductive function. We retained this name after we had been obliged by the findings of psychoanalysis to connect them less closely with reproduction. With the hypothesis of narcissistic libido and the extension of the concept of libido to the individual cells, the sexual drive was transformed for us into Eros, which seeks to force together and hold together the portions of living substance. What are commonly called the sexual instincts are looked upon as the part of Eros which is directed to objects. Our speculations have suggested that Eros operates from the beginning of life and appears as a "life instinct" in opposition to the death instinct which was brought into being by the coming to life of inorganic substance.
>
> (pp. 60–61)

In "Beyond The Pleasure Principle," Freud underscores the repetition compulsion and the insight that there are pleasures beyond the general pleasure principle. The force beyond the pleasure principle insists in restoring "an earlier state of things" (p. 57) – and what Freud means is a return to the state of the inorganic. It is this compulsion to repeat "which first puts us on the track of the death instincts" (p. 56). Here, Freud realizes for the first time that primary masochism may be at work and that the instinct that turns from the object to the ego may precede the instinct that turns from the ego to the object. In that context, Freud cites Sabina Spielrein as the one being instrumental in realizing that a destructive impulse is part and parcel of a creative impulse, so much that the act of construction is based on an act of destruction and that the one cannot really be separated from the other (Spielrein, 1912).

In the final section of "Beyond the Pleasure Principle," Freud makes some of his most radical statements about the death drive, which he will elaborate upon again in "The Ego and the Id" (1923). He says, almost in passing, that

> another striking fact is that the life instincts have so much more contact with our internal perceptions – emerging as breakers of peace and constantly producing tensions whose release is felt as pleasure – while the death instincts seems to do their work unobtrusively. The pleasure principle seems actually to serve the death instincts.
>
> (p. 63)

In "The Ego and the Id," Freud continues to refine this account and describes the death drive as being "mute" and being linked to melancholia while "the clamor of life proceeds for the most part from Eros" (1923, p. 46). The death drive becomes more purposeful in Freud's mind; it has a free hand behind the scenes of the superego which he now describes as a gathering place of the death drives. In regard to melancholia, Freud observes that

> the destructive component had entrenched itself in the super-ego and turned itself against the ego. What is now holding sway in the superego is, as it were, a pure culture of the death instinct, and in fact, it often enough succeeds in driving the ego into death, if the latter doesn't fend off its tyrant in time by the change round into mania.
>
> (p. 53)

In "The Economic Problem of Masochism" (1924), Freud elaborates not only upon the "pure culture of the death instinct" that resides in the superego, but he now focuses his attention on what is hiding underneath the shadow of the ego. He writes that "the libido meets the instinct of death, or destruction" (p. 163) in the multicellular organisms and that its task is to render the destructive component "innocuous . . . by diverting that instinct to a great extent outwards . . . towards objects in the external world. This instinct is then called the destructive instinct, the instinct for mastery, or the will to power" (p. 163). However, and here Freud takes a remarkable turn and asserts that, "Another portion does not share in this transposition outwards, it remains inside the organism and, with the help of the accompanying excitation . . . becomes libidinally bound there. It is in this portion that we have to recognize the original, erotogenic masochism" (p. 164). The melancholic serves as an example case for the masochistic, internal workings of the death drive, since the sadism of the superego and the masochism of the ego join forces, complementing each other and uniting themselves with one another in acting against the influences of the outside world. One could describe this dynamic as an internal "love fest" of destruction which defends itself against any intervention from the outside. Or, in the words of Freud,

> it may be said that the death drive which is operative in the organism – primal sadism – is identical with masochism. After the main portion of it has been transposed outwards to objects, there remains inside, as a residuum of it, the erotogenic masochism proper, which on the one hand has become a component of the libido and, on the other, still has the self as its object. The masochism would thus be evidence of, and a remainder from, the phase of development in which the coalescence, which is so important for life, between the death instinct and Eros took place.
>
> (1924, p. 163)[2]

Karl Abraham, as Bernard Toboul reminds us,

> had warned of the range of enjoyment that lies hidden behind the state of melancholy. In Freud's work of 1924 about *The Economic Problem of Masochism*, a formula will develop which shows the dimension of a ruinous jouissance, of the rejected object: the jouissance of the ruin of the self.
>
> (2013, p. 75, translation mine)

Freud in "Why War?" (1933), the last text in which he discusses the death drive before his final statements about it in "Analysis Terminable and Interminable" (1937), insists that Eros and Thanatos are inseparable and that the "phenomena of life arise from concurrent or mutually opposing action of both" (1933, p. 209). He argues that the instincts "do not operate in isolation" and that the self-preservative instinct has erotic features but

> must nevertheless have aggressiveness at its disposal to fulfill its purpose. So the instinct of love, when it is directed towards the object, stands in need for some contribution from the instinct of mastery if it is in any way to obtain possession of that object. The difficulty of isolating the two classes of instincts in their actual manifestations is indeed what has so long prevented us from recognizing them.
>
> (p. 210)

This essential realization was not heeded by most of Freud's followers however; either they ignored the life and death drive altogether, or they isolated the two drives, privileging in particular the destructive aspect of the death drive. Melanie Klein, for example, retained the death drive but focused primarily and almost exclusively on its destructive nature, which manifests itself in jealousy, greed, and envy and is also seen to be powerfully at work in the baby's early annihilation fears and terrors. She neglected, I believe, the double-sided nature of the death drive and its interweaving link with Eros, which, as Freud wrote, informs the "multiplicity of the phenomena of life." (Only by the concurrent or mutually opposing action of the two primal instincts – Eros and the death instinct – never by one or the other alone, can we explain the rich multiplicity of the phenomena of life.) Thus Klein's use of the concept reduces the complexity of the dynamics of the death drive and transforms it into a purely destructive force directed primarily at an external object. In contrast, I think, Jacques Lacan took on Freud's theory of the death drive in all of its complexity, emphasizing the libidinal aspect of the death drive, as it becomes the source for the pleasure in the destruction of the self. Lacan placed the death drive at the centre of his entire theoretical and clinical body of work. The sovereignty and power of the death and life drive can be detected in many of Lacan's writings, be it in his conception of the Real, the register of the unsymbolizable, or his re-definition of trauma, but, I think, he expresses it most powerfully in his theory of *jouissance*, which is the pleasure/lust that goes beyond the limit and is experienced in its excess as both exceedingly pleasurable and painful, turning its pursuit of pleasure into an abyss of tension and pain. For Lacan, the essential point was that the repetition compulsion that Freud had described in "The Uncanny" (1919) and "Beyond the Pleasure Principle" (1920) was to be found in the transference, in the symptom, and in the dynamics of anxiety.

While the mere movement of repetition is central to the pleasure principle, what is at stake in the repetition compulsion is the daemonic power that overrides the pleasure principle, going beyond it and *seeking a torturous, often, self-ruinous pleasure for its own sake*. Lacan's *jouissance* is perhaps most closely aligned to Freud's erotogenic masochism (1924, p. 164) as he describes it in "The Economic Problem of Masochism" when he writes that "even the subject's destruction of himself cannot take place without libidinal satisfaction" (1924, p. 170).

Lacan shifts away from an emphasis upon death to a focus upon the repetitive nature of *jouissance* which balances itself off against desire and is embedded in both pleasure and unpleasure, suffering and ecstasy. He no longer needs to differentiate between pleasure and unpleasure, because both are combined in the workings of *jouissance*. This shift in Lacan's work is essential, because it no longer suggests a simple and seemingly clear division between pleasure and unpleasure, between a life and a death drive, but instead endorses the idea that the death drive appears in guise (*Psychischen Umkleidung*; see Freud, 1924, p. 165) of a pleasurable addiction to suffering. With Freud's "Beyond the Pleasure Principle," both the theoretical and clinical discussion have changed, since the phenomena of a negative therapeutic reaction, of masochism, of anorexia, of addictions and the repetition of trauma illustrate that there is a powerful force at work in the unconscious which Freud called "daemonic" and which Lacan defines as "jouissance" that wants to derive pleasure at any and all costs, no matter how painful, torturous, or exhilarating that pursuit may be. While Lacan initially conceptualized a symptom to be a purely linguistic phenomenon, a message that was written into the body, ready to be deciphered by the Other, Lacan, by following Freud's tracks, realized that the bodily symptom does not readily dissolve but instead stubbornly refuses to be reached by words. This realization led Lacan to define *jouissance* as excess pleasure/tension residing at the core of each symptom. Every subject is deeply attached to his/her symptom or addiction because it is the symptom that provides an auto-erotic/self-preservative and deadly unconscious source of painful pleasure that the subject is loath to sacrifice. Every prohibition, every limit creates the desire to transgress it, without a law there would be no desire, and as such, *jouissance* is the force that is always bound to transgress no matter what the consequences are. The death drive, according to Dylan Evans, is "the name given to that constant desire in the subject to break through the pleasure principle" (1996, p. 92). For the path towards death is nothing other than what is called *jouissance*.

In the end, we can see how the death drive did not simply constitute an aberration of Freud's psychoanalytic theory but proved itself to be a concept with a complex pre-history and with an intricate post-Freudian history, one that is still influencing current clinical work and contemporary theoretical thought.

Notes

1   How truly grateful and indebted Freud found himself to be to the work of Empedocles, is, I believe, symbolized in the fact that the four elements Empedocles speaks about, "earth, air, fire, and water," are given great prominence in Freud's waiting room where four etchings hang over the "waiting couch," illustrating the four competing forces/elements .
2   See for further discussion, Bernard Toboul's article, *Psychose maniaco-dépressive et psychanalyse* (2013, pp. 73–91).

References

Evans, D. (1996). *Dictionary of Lacanian Psychoanalysis*. London: Routledge.

Freud, S. (1900). *The Interpretation of Dreams*. Standard Edition 4 & 5.

Freud, S. (1905). *Three Essays on the Theory of Sexuality*. Standard Edition 7.

Freud, S. (1910). *The Psycho-Analytic View of Psychogenic Disturbance of Vision*. Standard Edition 11:209–218.

Freud, S. (1914). *On Narcissism: An Introduction*. Standard Edition 14:67–102.

Freud, S. (1917 [1915]). *Mourning and Melancholia*. Standard Edition 14:237–258.

Freud, S. (1919). *The Uncanny*. Standard Edition 17:217–256.

Freud, S. (1920). *Beyond the Pleasure Principle*. Standard Edition 18:1–64.

Freud, S. (1923). *The Ego and the Id*. Standard Edition 19:1–66.

Freud, S. (1924). *The Economic Problem of Masochism*. Standard Edition 19:155–170.

Freud, S. (1933). *Why War?* Standard Edition 22:195–216.

Freud, S. (1937). *Analysis Terminable and Interminable*. Standard Edition 23:209–254.

Freud, S. (1950 [1895]). *Project for a Scientific Psychology*. Standard Edition 1:281–391.

Spielrein, S. (1912). Destruction as a cause of coming into being. Trans. K. McCormick (1994). *Journal of Analytical Psychology, 39*:155–186. Originally: *Jahrbuch für psychoanalytische und psychopathologische Forschungen, 4*:465–504.

Toboul, B. (2013). Psychose maniaco-dépressive et psychanalyse. *Figures de la Psychanalyse, 26*:73–91. Paris: Erès.

PART II
CLINICAL ASPECTS

CHAPTER 4

Is the death drive mute – or do we pretend to be deaf?

Sylvia Zwettler-Otte

*Introductory remarks about the death drive and how to translate "*Trieb*"*

The death drive is a difficult and controversially discussed theme. Freud's hypothesis about the life and death drives is best understood as a conceptual framework that may be helpful in terms of detecting and grasping unconscious ideas, thus "putting theory to work" in our clinical practice. We use concepts that are illuminating and useful as "both public or private theories" (Canestri, 2012, p. XXIII). Such theories form a network that is dense and airy at the same time. In this way, it is possible to connect the personal experiences of the analyst with the strong ropes of theory (cf. Zwettler-Otte, 2011b, p. 10).

The term "death drive" as opposed to "death instinct" is closer to Freud's original German term *Trieb*. As Arthur Goldschmidt (2005, pp. 15–33) has shown, *Trieb* (drive) derives from the verb "*treiben*" and literally means impelling a quick movement or chasing. Whether one has a definite goal is not the issue: one may move with or without a definite goal. Freud referred for instance to *Trieb* as a "quota of energy, which presses in a particular direction" (Freud, 1933, p. 35).

In his paper "Making Contact with the Primitive Mind," Sebastian J. Kohon (2014, pp. 245–270) explores Bion's notion of a contact-barrier and the latter's relation to Freud's drive theory. Referring to Strachey's translation of Freud's term "*Trieb*" as "instinct" rather than "drive" and to Ron Britton's description of Freud's use of the terms *Trieb* and *Instinkt*, Kohon takes up Britton's question whether *Trieb* and *Instinkt* are two different innate forces and comes to the conclusion "that Freud *can* be understood as referring to two different and opposing forces" (p. 264) original emphasis). Kohon links Freud's remark about *instinct* as a "hardly definable knowledge, something, as it were, preparatory to an understanding" (Freud, 1918, p. 120) to Bion's notion of preconception as an innate capacity to have a phantasy. In other words, instinct might describe "a tendency that 'seeks' to structure the mind." *Drive*, on the other hand, describes impulses "that 'seek' radically to transgress boundaries, to push through, to remain formless."

Freud sometimes uses the singular, sometimes the plural tense to refer to *Trieb*. For instance, in "The Ego and the Id" he writes: "the death instincts are by their nature mute" (Freud, 1923, p. 46) – in the German original text "daß die Todestriebe im wesentlichen stumm sind." I will use the singular tense, thus focusing on the force itself behind the plurality of figures and forms.

The term "death drive" or "*Todestrieb*" contains in a single word what is irritating about the concept as such. We are here faced with the dialectic of life and death: death means stopping life, whereas drive means pushing it forward (cf. Pontalis, 1998, p. 216). Indeed, in analysis we are confronted with the result of these opposed forces in a vacillating rhythm ("*Zauderrhythmus*").

I cannot see how this dialectic of opposed forces can be evaded in our clinical work or our theoretical conceptions. Without this dialectic, it is impossible to develop a sensibility for the essential conflicts between the conscious and the unconscious, between repression and the return of the repressed, between the desired and the uncanny, and between the drive for knowledge and the *passion for ignorance*. As Gregorio Kohon has succinctly put it: "This is fully demonstrated in every session, every day, by the patient on the couch . . . after all, it is the patient's unconscious resistance to knowledge which allows psychoanalytic treatment to happen" (Kohon G., 1999, p. 156f.). He refers to the *drive for knowledge* as one form of love, first described by Freud in the case of Little Hans (1909a) as infantile *sexual curiosity* and soon thereafter in the case of the

Rat Man (1909b as *epistemophilic instinct* (Kohon G., 1999, p. 156f.). Once again, we are confronted with Eros and Thanatos.

Several great psychoanalytic thinkers, among them J.-B. Pontalis and André Green, have emphasized that Freud's concept of the death drive is as constitutive for psychoanalysis as is the concept of sexuality. However, in practice, it is often easier to recognize the binding of Eros than it is to recognize the unbinding of the death drive. The death drive operates silently inside the individual. According to Freud, when this drive is directed outwards, against objects, it constitutes destructiveness or aggressiveness. In other words, the death drive starts inside the individual, may turn outwards, but also inwards once again. A death wish may translate into a wish to destroy an object, or it may be directed against the act of wishing itself. In the latter case, we are confronted with the annihilation of desire per se. Instead of seeking to satisfy a need, the subject steered by the death drive ends up killing all those activities that Hanna Segal called "life-promoting" (1993, p. 55).

In "Civilization and Its Discontents" Freud gave a simple and yet accurate statement about the life-death drive concepts: he wrote that initially he had advanced his views only tentatively,

> but in the course of time they have gained such a hold upon me that I can no longer think in any other way. To my mind, they are far more serviceable from a theoretical standpoint than any other possible ones; *they provide that simplification, without either ignoring or doing violence to the facts, for which we strive in scientific work.*
>
> (Freud, 1930, p. 119, own emphasis)

The case of a 35-year-old man "without any private life"

I now want to present the analysis of a young man (five times a week). I will focus on some manifestations of the death drive and the severe problems attached to these: the loud and silent versions and forms of destruction and aggression that I was sometimes not ready to hear. The death drive expressed itself in attacks on linking (Bion) in external relationships and in the transference. It also expressed itself in decathexis and disobjectalization (Green), as well as in attacks against the setting, which led to long periods during which the patient lost access to his dreams, and to a serious crisis after three years of analysis.

The patient, whom I will here refer to by the name of Ralph, is today 35 years old. He was an excellent pupil and student and is now very successful in his profession. But he has, as he says, "no private life at all." Four years ago, during the summer holidays, he became intensely depressed and anxious about having a breakdown. At the hospital, where he was brought by his father, he received medication and was recommended intensive psychotherapy. Ralph's father went out to search for an analyst and contacted someone he had once heard giving a lecture who had impressed him. My colleague considered the urge of the father a bad start and referred him to me, mentioning that the son would have to call me himself, which Ralph eventually did.

My first impression of Ralph during the initial interview was that he was much younger. Had he not been dressed in an elegant suit, I would have thought him a young man just about to begin his university studies. He spoke of his expanding feeling of emptiness, which dated back to the period of his studies, about his lonely weekends spent at home, lying in bed, and about his hopelessness about finding a woman who might be interested in him. He underlined that *she* would have to be interested in him. It did not occur to him that he might himself be interested in someone! This attitude was nonetheless contradicted by his narrative. He recounted an incident that had occurred four years earlier. At that time, he had decided to travel to another country to visit a female colleague, whom he had got to know superficially a year earlier. Much to his chagrin, considering the great expectations he had attached to the journey, she could hardly remember him. When I asked, whether this incident did not, in fact, take place shortly before his first anxiety breakout, he was astonished about the link. He then recalled a similar incident at the end of high school when he had helped a classmate with the final exam. Then, like now, he had been disappointed because she only thanked him verbally, giving him neither a kiss nor a hug. I was thus made aware of how he tended to become disappointed in women and had to ask myself whether he was now perhaps also sceptical about me, not least since he had originally expected to work together with a male analyst. "Never mind," he said in a disinterested voice. I had yet to become aware how this "never mind" would materialize in the transference.

During the first year of analysis I simply did not exist in Ralph's mind. Four times a week he went straight to the couch, avoiding even to look at me. However, after weekends as well as on Thursdays (we had at the time no session on Wednesday) he felt very confused, trying desperately to remember what had happened during the previous session. "The psychoanalytic setting, with its regularity of time and place, the supporting couch" and the "crucial factor" of my efforts to understand him (Segal, 1993, p. 53) had provided some containment making it possible for some unconscious material to emerge. But this remained rather disintegrated and uncontained for some time. Consequently, he continued to despair about falling into a void. This was the reason why we decided to add a fifth session. There followed a phase of disclosure with many of the memories and details of his everyday life.

He talked about his cousin with whom he had played as a child; about the intense quarrelling between his parents, both teachers; the furious scenes staged by his mother and his father's withdrawal; and about how he himself managed to become like a stone wall when his mother slapped him because of some disobedience or lack of perfection. He had decided not to feel anything!

He erected this stone wall in the transference as well – and it was as thick as a fortress. Even when complaining profusely at the beginning of each week or after holidays about his hopeless loneliness and his feeling of emptiness, he was not prepared to admit that he may have missed his sessions, let alone me. This was not only an attack on linking as postulated by Bion. His fortress had been there right from the start and was used to keep me out and everyone else too. Only gradually did he realize that his pride about his narcissistic triumph of invulnerability was an obstacle regarding his longing for closeness. In very weak moments he would admit, "There may be some truth in what you are saying." One such occasion was when I tried to show him the conflict between his conscious desire to overcome loneliness and his unconscious attack of all occasions for getting into contact with others – both professionally and in his private life.

He realized his enormous fear of the analytical relationship when his cousin, who knew from his parents that he was in analysis with me, gave him one of my books to read (the German version of *The Melody of Separation*; Zwettler-Otte, 2011a). He returned the book immediately and came to his session in distress. His disconcerting feelings confused him. He said nobody should know me, nobody should know about his problems, and more so, he hated being forced to think of me, as he put it, and to have seen a chapter in the book, he would perhaps have liked to read.

I saw these and other signs that Eros had planted in Ralph's mind. Ralph began to bring his dreams to analysis and was gradually able to use them to begin to gain some control over his inner chaos. His tendency to moan about his loneliness began to lessen as he recognized his masochistic pleasure in this.

Another interesting detail from this phase concerned his politeness. At the end of the sessions we shook hands, as is usual here in Vienna, and he would always say "Danke" – thank you. His "thank you," however, was illustrative of the splitting described by Betty Joseph as characteristic of patients, "who seem apparently highly co-operative and adult, but in whom this co-operation is a pseudo-cooperation aiming at keeping the analyst away from the real unknown and more needy infantile parts of the self" (Joseph, 1997, p. 76). Winnicott talked in this connection of the "false self." This is how Ralph was at the beginning. But over time, his "thank you" began to feel differently. Sometimes, after productive sessions, it felt serious and authentic. At other times, it was just polite and false. Occasionally, he said nothing at all.

While passivity and withdrawal were silent ways of destruction, there were louder ones as well: Ralph began to regularly call his father on Fridays to tell him he was desperate and needed to see him. The father would leave his wife and Ralph's mother alone to come to meet his son, often driving a long way. This was a successful blow against both parents, who were concerned and helpless. It is remarkable that when Ralph was desperate, he never called his mother, but always his father, whom he experienced as more caring. He had somehow changed his father's gender, an unconscious process, which was determined in contradictory ways. On the surface, it is easy to understand that he felt more attracted to the parent he perceived as both kinder and as more reliable. But given Ralph's severe disturbance, and considering his difficulties with respect to reaching the stage of erotic differentiation, his need for his father resembled a relationship to a primary object belonging to the pre-oedipal phase of development (cf. Guex, 2015, pp. 46ff).

At another level, however – and later in analysis in the sense of *Nachträglichkeit* – his conversion of the father into a maternal figure stood for his wish to castrate his father. For the first time, Ralph experienced rage against his parents. In his phantasy, his mother was transformed into a fury while his father became an impotent slack. Thus transformed, Ralph's parents had to atone, together and in a double sense, for his bad childhood. They were supposed to feel guilt and pay for his analysis. This was remarkable considering that Ralph had a high income. He referred to his Friday calls to his father as "cries for help," yet these were filled with hatred. When these finally became more seldom, he turned his anger against me: I had spoiled his little satisfactions with my interpretations, which disturbed his rage against his parents as well as his weekend regression to a state uninhabited by desire. Sadistic, secret revenge or regressive apathy became his favourite destructive expressions. He either killed his objects or he killed his wish for love. In parallel he continued to seek partial gratification of his needs by way of blurred symbiotic phantasies that required no other object.

Instead of seeking out opportunities for satisfaction (Segal, 1993, p. 55) with an object, with whom he could find a way out of his loneliness, Ralph withdrew into deep regression nearly every weekend, immersing himself in a kind of oceanic feeling that vaguely resembled fusion, albeit without an object in sight. Or, he annihilated any need, devoted to a "desire for not-desire," as Aulagnier put it (Aulagnier, 1975, cited in Feurer, 2007, p. 444). This came close to "an aspiration for the level zero," a characterization used by André Green (2005, p. 222) to describe *negative narcissism* as an expression of the *disobjectalizing function*, that is to say of the destruction of an object through disinvestment. Ralph engaged in this type of destruction whenever I addressed his transference feelings. He insisted I was no real person. "That's the analytic method, the analyst being invisible and non-existent," he once claimed whilst adding: "I could never tolerate another method."

Before starting analysis, Ralph's sexual experiences were limited to encounters with prostitutes. This had brought him some relief with regard to his narcissistic concern whether "it worked." But these dates did not make him happy and he seemed surprised about this. During the second year of analysis he dated female colleagues but withdrew every time when either his interest found some echo or her interest felt too strong. Once he reported a touching scene: he had tried to explain to a young and attractive woman, whom he had invited for dinner and whom he had begun to like, why he did not wish to have a dog: the dog would always be there! Both of them realized that it was not only dogs he experienced as threatening. Nothing should impinge on his exclusive inner world.

Ralph's way of speaking had been striking from the very first session: he always spoke very slowly, seemingly searching for the perfect and best wording. In fact, he was very reluctant about following the fundamental rule and rejected many of his associations, convinced that what had come to his mind would lead us nowhere. This was part of his attack on analysis. But as Michael Parsons recently argued, free association is "more than an extended process of resolving resistances and the conflicts that provoke them" (Parsons, 2016). Referring to Christopher Bollas, Parsons points to the significance of allowing a multiplicity of ideas to emerge into consciousness, the revelation of significance in the midst of confusion, and to the deeply satisfying experience associated with the discovery of a new richness and texture in a patient's thinking. He also mentions Green "notion of free association as a radiating, not a linear process that produces a continually ramifying, ever more complex 'arborescent' structure of thought" (Parsons, 2016, p. 7f). At this point Parsons turns to the death drive that destroys structure and organization by inhibiting that fresh energy is injected into a system, dissolving it "until eventually it has no structure left at all . . . the more a system loses its complexity, the closer it comes to a random state where its structure has ceased to exist" (Parsons, 2016, p. 7f). Seen from this perspective, Ralph's analysis was not only about *freeing him from* his suffering, but also about *freeing him to* increase psychic complexity and to become more fully alive.

He had cut off all ways of being touched. After graduating he had stopped reading anything that was not linked to his profession. Several times he mentioned that while still at school he had devoured Arthur Schnitzler. Although Ralph thought it would be nice to go to the theatre or to an exhibition, he never did. Culture did not bring him comfort or encouragement but was experienced as uncanny. As Gregorio Kohon wrote about aesthetic experience:

> this is what the Freudian uncanny represents in the aesthetic: an encounter with the negative, something secret or repressed in the subject, which the artistic or literary object has brought to light or around which it is at least circling, threatening to do so.
>
> (Kohon G., 2016, p. 150)

Even when Ralph sat hours in front of the television, most of the time he avoided watching any films. He only mentioned once at the end of a session that he could not stop himself from watching a film about a man, who instead of growing older became younger, to finally die as a baby in the arms of his girlfriend. I was alarmed about his fascination with regression and his strong longing for finding back to the primary object. Nevertheless, although the only phantasy that spoke to him was a regressive one, regression was a movement and I inclined to prefer this to his stasis. Dana Birksted-Breen has written: "Pathology takes over when 'stuckness' predominates, and it is with this that Freud became preoccupied when he introduced the notion of the death drive" (Birksted-Breen, 2016, p. 4). Ralph's efforts to avoid the penumbra of nearly all representations of mental states did not protect him from despair: "Non-representation is experienced by the ego as an excess of excitation, and if the mind does not arrive, by virtue of a transformation, at an experience of intelligibility accessible to the system of representation, the ego will experience it as traumatic" (Botella & Botella, 2005, p. 113).

Ralph experienced being without a loving partner as traumatic. Once a colleague, who wanted to discuss with him a project, persuaded Ralph to join him and his little son for a visit to the zoo; next day he told me he could imagine becoming interested in animals. But this idea, like all others before, quickly evaporated behind his dominant complaints about being alone. This attitude reminded me of Reiter consideration of the death drive as an effort to grasp the uncanny of the biological side of life and to find a psychological language for the narcissistic wound inflicted by the realization that in the natural history of genus, an individual is but a quantity to be neglected (Reiter, 1996). Nature for Ralph did not represent a holding mother but rather a rigid and hard one, like his own mother, who in his view was more interested in her school children than in him. He was then jealous for the first time, realizing at the same time how much he had suffered when his mother had started again to work as a teacher when he was three years old.

In the transference the provocations became stronger. Ralph treated me either as the kind, but impotent father, who was unable to help him, or as the bad mother, who sticks coldly to the rules of the setting instead of letting him come and go whenever he pleases. Now in the fourth year of analysis he attacked the setting seriously, coming very late every morning, often sacrificing half of his time, still in heavy resistance against his feelings and often withdrawn in his fortress. In a way, this paralleled his experiences during the fourth year of his life, when he faced strange attacks of paralysis. His parents had brought him to hospital, where no somatic cause was detected.

I was concerned that stasis might now take over also in "the analytic situation itself becoming a pathological organisation 'à deux' in

which primitive anxieties and movements are avoided for fear of collapse, or in which the trauma is relived without any modification"
(Birksted-Breen, 2016, p. 4). I wondered whether in my countertransference I had become now the helplessly concerned father as a
substitute for the rigid or absent mother. However, it was exactly this
experience of being helpless and lost that forced me to confront the
dangerous passivity and silent unbinding of the death drive. Maybe I
had missed some low tones in what my patient was telling me. I was
perhaps too busy keeping note of the signs of Eros, following Ralph,
who was struggling to turn away from the holes Thanatos had dug. It
was necessary to become infected with the patient's horror. Only then
could we dare take a closer look at it, making it possible for Ralph to
slowly give up his attacks against the setting and begin using again
the full time of analysis. To share the horror of the manifestations of
the death drive – the passivity of being stuck, the dissolving of hope
and meaning, the disobjectalization etc. – experienced by both of us,
patient and analyst, was a precondition for activating the life drive
again in us both (cf. Beland, 2011).

Ralph's analysis is still a work in progress. It is not yet a report of
a victory but rather one from the battlefield against the death drive.
The clinical material helps us to see some essential characteristics of the
death drive:

- There is at present, in this patient's life no object that is libidinally
  invested. André Green considered Freud's concept of the binding
  life drive and the unbinding death drive "sound but insufficient"
  (Green, 1999, p. 85). He tried to complete Freud's death drive theory by advancing the idea of a disobjectalizing function. Ralph is
  a patient suffering from a withdrawal of investment. His perfec-
  tionism at work and his sophisticated way of speaking may be
  residues of former libidinal investments that have been destroyed
  long ago.
- Green's hypothesis of a negative narcissism may also explain the
  patient's extreme passivity, which he is only able to suspend at
  work. This passivity is his "stonewall," a fortress he defends with
  all his strength. This not only destroys links, but also inhibits their
  potential development.
- Whenever this patient turns his destructive impulses outwards,
  something he does successfully at work, hate comes to the fore.

- What has remained from his capacity to love is a desperate, formless desire, for which he cannot find an object. He also has no representation or conscious phantasy in this regard.
- His relationship to his parents suggests he may have faced severe problems in his relationship to his mother as the primary object. As a result, he continually demands motherly features in his father. An oedipal rivalry began to emerge in his dreams only recently.
- In the transference positive feelings are concealed. Instead, he assigns to me the helpless role of his father or that of the hostile mother with whom he fights. However, neither he nor I wish to resign. We are intent on overcoming his sadomasochism.
- Over a period of several months the patient could not express his inner struggles other than by attacking the setting and cutting down the sessions. It was important, it seems, that I should come to realize the full extent of threatening annihilation he is living with in the countertransference. This enabled containment and understanding and helped reawaken the patient's readiness to communicate and understand.

The difficulties to detect and bear the destructive and dissolving activities in analysis are often experienced by patients as a repeated failure of containment. In this context, acting in or out become emergency exits, representing efforts to communicate the fear of and even the wish for annihilation. *The analyst's resistance to take these overwhelming experiences in might be considered as reluctance to listen to the low but powerful voices of the death drive. This gave my chapter the title: Is the death drive mute – or do we pretend to be deaf?*

In an effort to assess the usefulness of Freud's concept of the death drive, Hermann Beland (2011) discussed clinical and theoretical examples of Freud, Segal, Bion, and Rosenfeld as well as his own. His own case vignette exemplifies impressively how the analyst's experience of the manifestation of the death drive is often unconscious and primarily not a conscious act. Beland's reaction was embedded in the withdrawal of his hand when his female patient, upon leaving, and as they were shaking hands, said she was convinced he was a bad ghost who would finally destroy her. His spontaneous gesture of withdrawing his hand *more quickly than the patient herself* was an act of separation, an answer only to her words. In the next session he could tell the patient what he understood subsequently: in fact, what had happened was that the patient had for the first time shown her affection for him, acknowledging the joint work and her hope to receive and be able to accept help despite the paranoia that infected her thoughts. In the hand-shaking scene she unconsciously demonstrated both her intention to destroy herself, projected onto the analyst, and her wish for cure holding on to his hand. There was, on the one hand, a split in her relationship to her analyst and an attempt at intimidation. This is what her words expressed. On the other hand, by telling these words while shaking hands she was at the same time unconsciously trying to integrate her extreme ambivalence, thus also expressing the wish he would manage to hold onto her despite her hostility. Beland recognized that the confrontation with the concentrated projection of the self-destructive intention, the manifestation of the death drive, activated the patient's but also his own life drive, resulting in therapeutic hope.

In the case of Ralph, there was no short and unexpected scene helping us detect and experience the full and undeniable extent of the work of the negative. Rather, over a protracted period of time, he attacked the setting to such a degree that analytic work seemed almost impossible. This led to an escalation of the patient's despair and to serious doubts on my part whether this crisis could be resolved. Eventually, however, it was possible to contain and understand the horrible struggle between destructive unbinding and constructive, binding forces. I managed to win the patient's trust by paying careful attention to his emerging capacity for new positive feelings.

Repressed intentions play out in different ways. They sometimes materialize as in a flash of a discharging action like the spontaneous withdrawal of Beland's hand. At other times they lurk in the background, creeping in, at first unnoticed, eventually causing a vague and increasingly disturbing sense of discontent (Zwettler-Otte, 2014). Both mechanisms must be understood and translated into the patient's language.

Arthur Schnitzler's novel Dying

In his puberty, my patient "devoured" Schnitzler's works. Thereafter, he cut off all access to literature or art. He may have read the novel *Dying*, which is an extraordinary representation of the battle between the life and death drive.

Freud always stressed the affinity, the close relationship, and the transitions between so called normal and pathological processes. The struggles between binding and unbinding forces, between Eros and Thanatos, are not limited to mental pathology; they are inherent in life and death. Therefore, I want to finish my considerations about the death drive with some comments on Arthur Schnitzler's novel *Dying*.

My aim is to show how much Arthur Schnitzler, a medical doctor and poet, already knew about destructiveness and the struggles between opposing forces in our inner world. He wrote the novel *Dying* (original "*Sterben*") in 1895 – the year of Freud and Breuer's publication of their "Studies in Hysteria" and of Freud's "Project of a Scientific Psychology." This was 25 years before Freud introduced the notion of the death drive in "Beyond the Pleasure Principle."

I have used this novel in my book *Melody of Separation* (Zwettler-Otte, 2011a) in order to illustrate a "healthy" process of mourning in Marie, the young woman, whose fiancé is going to die. Now I focus my attention on the work of dying in Felix, her fiancé.

Felix comes unusually late to the appointment with Marie, his fiancée, at the Augarten. He has just received the diagnosis he is suffering from a mortal disease and has at most a year to live. He chose to consult a famous medical expert because he suspected his own physician and friend Alfred was not telling him the truth. Felix is very reluctant to tell Marie, but she insists, and he finally tells her as they sit in a quiet garden restaurant of the Prater – a place they both like. He can hardly believe that "in a year I'll be lying cold in the ground, perhaps already rotting away" (Schnitzler, 1970, p. 16), while Marie will look just as now. He rejects Marie's desperate oath that she cannot live without him and wants to die with him: "I have no right to take you with me. [. . .] Don't swear anything. One day you'd be asking me to release you from your word. [. . .] I must go and you must stay" (pp. 19f.).

The next morning Felix exhibits this same brave attitude in a conversation with his doctor-friend Alfred: "All I have to think of at this point is how to spend my last year as wisely as possible" (p. 24). First signs of envy appear, when Felix speaks about Alfred's chance to live much longer than he. Following Alfred's advice, Felix and Marie rent a house in the mountains and hope that "here, in these new surroundings, the sentence of death pronounced in another world no longer held good" (p. 26). However, at the lake, looking up to the sky, "that terrible distance," makes Felix feel eerie. The scenery seems uncanny to him and he can no longer repress thoughts about his illness. He feels terribly defenceless. Rationalizations, philosophy, or jokes that "in fact the whole world is full of people condemned to death" (p. 31) do not help. Felix tries to face reality and mocks Marie, who seems unable to. He projects his difficulties onto her.

His narcissism looks for yet another proof of braveness: he will write a testament like a poem, leaving the whole beautiful world to Marie, a quiet, smiling farewell as a triumph. Shortly afterwards he can no longer grasp how ill he is: "the joy of his recovery had disguised itself as the desire to take a proud farewell of the world" (p. 37). Angrily he rejects Marie's remarks denying his illness. After a short time of passion, the distance between Marie and Felix grows, and there will now "undertones of indifference in him" (p. 41), signs of a withdrawal of investment. Felix starts to remind Marie of her oath to die with him. Realizing her helplessness, he fears she is beginning to hope it will soon all be over, and that, ultimately, she will be relieved when he dies. He observes her with mounting jealousy as they come across other young men in the village. His hate also turns against himself. He curses the day when he asked the famous medical doctor to tell him the truth about his merciless illness – about this he now speaks of as "false dignity" (p. 47). His love for Marie evaporates slowly as decathexis progresses: "it often seemed as if it wouldn't be so difficult to part from this creature after all. She was no longer a part of his essential being" (p. 48). She was no longer an individual for him, rather a possession that he could decide to take with him when he dies.

Interestingly, Schnitzler also envisages the idea of a double as observed by M'Uzan (2003) in dying patients, albeit displaced onto Marie who is split between her lover and her wish to survive. When Felix happens to read in the newspaper about the sudden death of the famous medical expert who had confirmed his gloomy diagnosis, he relives his hate against that man and takes his death as a favourable sign concerning himself. Felix begins to turn his destructiveness outwards as he experiences hate, envy, and jealousy against those who will go on living after he is gone. He loses interest in all that Marie is doing and wants to share with him. When for a moment a wish for happiness comes up, he no longer cares about sharing it with Marie. He reproaches her for being "too fond of life" (Schnitzler, 1970, p. 63). He calls her sarcastically his ministering angel and does not mind hurting her. He reproaches Alfred for not saving him and despises the philosophers who pretend to be brave and deny their fear of death, which he recognizes to be "as natural as dying itself" (p. 76). Once again, he accuses himself to be a liar. Towards the end, he is either indifferent or obsessed by his wish that Marie should die with him. For a while he is euphoric as he plans to travel to the South. He has no clear plans, but it was "like hearing the instruments of an orchestra tuning up" (p. 96). Briefly he considers travelling to Africa to produce a masterpiece there. But quickly he loses faith and is unable to experience any pleasure. In the last scene of the novel Marie runs out of the house, seeking escape, as he puts her under pressure with his wish that she should not let him die alone. She returns with Alfred. Felix sees her with another man and in his imagination this other man is immensely tall. Then everything around him starts to rotate as if dancing to a wonderful music. He falls out of the window.

The novel *Dying* shows how the young man Felix tries to cope with the diagnosis of his fatal illness. This confirmation of an earlier vague fear is itself a traumatic experience that causes profound deconstructing and decathexis (Laub & Lee, 2003, p. 433).

We become witnesses of the dramatic process of disinvestment, defusion of the drives, disobjectalization, and decathexis. His inner world is dominated by destructive feelings like envy and jealousy against all those that will still be alive after he is gone. He uses philosophy to fight against the uncanny fear of death and becomes immersed in narcissistic phantasies about a sovereign farewell, like writing a last will in the form of a poem. He projects and attacks his own incapacity to cope with the fatal situation onto Marie, whereby his and her coping difficulties with this unbearable situation get blurred, and he turns all his anger and hostility against Alfred, who is a friend of both of them. Destructiveness turns outwards and against himself. Silent indifference and loud hate alternate with each other. Despair, envy, and jealousy towards those who will presumably go on living are followed by voids. Manic ideas of producing a masterpiece collapse rather quickly as the binding forces weaken. Felix becomes more and more obsessed by the symbiotic wish to die together with Marie, although he is no longer meaningfully related to her as a result of the growing withdrawal of cathexis; he is now hardly able to feel a difference between her and other young women. The vivid fight between the life drive and the triumphant death drive ends in the happy delusion of a dance to wonderful music: Felix is ready to throw himself in the arms of Marie and Alfred, who now appear to him as immensely tall figures (protecting parents?). He falls into death. This dance into death may represent the submission of the pleasure principle to the service of the death drive, a final revival of the life drive to facilitate the unavoidable last step.

Conclusion

I began this chapter by explicating why Freud's notion of the "*Todes-trieb*" is better translated as *death drive* rather than *death instinct*: death *drive* conveys the idea of a primitive force pressing "in a particular direction" (Freud, 1933, p. 95), transgressing boundaries and remaining formless, while *instinct* entails a progressive aspect seeking to structure the mind, developing and making use of an innate capacity that prepares an understanding (Kohon S. J., 2014, p. 264).

I demonstrated the clinical usefulness of Freud's life and death drive concept using clinical material from an analysis of a young man (five times a week). I showed some manifestations of the death drive and the severe problems they cause: the loud and silent versions and forms of destruction and aggression, the attacks on linking in the transference and in external relationships, the decathexis and disobjectalization, the long periods of losing access to dreams, and a serious crisis after three years of analysis. To overcome the risk of the patient's stasis taking over, it seemed important to experience in the countertransference the full extent of this destructive force, followed by a better understanding and a new rise of the life drive as a resurrected therapeutic hope.

While my patient suffered from a kind of emotional anorexia regarding culture and could only remember that as an adolescent he used to be fond of Arthur Schnitzler, I use Schnitzler's novella *Dying*, written in 1895, to demonstrate the workings of the death drive outside what we call psychic pathology. The novel deals with the death of a young man who tells his fiancée about the diagnosis of his fatal disease. We can detect there many manifestations of the death drive: the confrontation with and repression of unbearable reality, the battle between caring love and its progressive withdrawal, helpless efforts to cope with the incurable narcissistic wound by way of triumph and proof of strength, increasing apathy alternating with destructive feelings that are turned outwards as envy and jealousy, and finally, having lost nearly all libidinal energy, a lethal symbiotic delusion of dancing into a union with the parents.

References

Aulagnier, P. (1975). *La Violence de l'Interpretation*. Paris: Presses Universitaires de France.

Birksted-Breen, D. (2016). *The Work of Psychoanalysis: Sexuality, Time and the Psychoanalytic Mind*. London: Routledge.

Beland, H. (2011). Erklärungs- und Arbeitswert der Todestriebhypothese. Diskussion anhand klinischer und theoretischer Beispiele [The explanatory and clinical usefulness of the concept of death instinct: Discussion of clinical and theoretical examples of some of its representatives]. In: H. Beland (Eds.), *Unaushaltbarkeit, Psychoanalytische Aufsätze II* (pp. 145–166). Jahrbuch der Psychoanalyse, 56:23–47.

Botella, C., & Botella, S. (2005). *The Work of Psychic Figurability: Mental States without Representation*. Hove: Brunner Routledge.

Canestri, J. (Ed.) (2012). *Putting Theory to Work*. London: Karnac.

Feurer, M. (2007). Repräsentation und Denken bei Piera Aulagnier [Piera Aulagnier on thinking and representation]. *Zeitschrift für psychoanalytische Theorie und Praxis, 22*:443–461.

Freud, S. (1909a). *Analysis of a phobia in a five-year-old-boy*. Standard Edition 10.

Freud, S. (1909b). *Notes upon a case of obsessional neurosis*. Standard Edition 10.

Freud, S. (1923). *The Ego and the Id*. Standard Edition 19:1–66.

Freud, S. (1930). *Civilization and Its Discontents*. Standard Edition 21:57–146.

Freud, S. (1933). *New Introductory Lectures on Psycho-Analysis*. Standard Edition 22:1–182.

Goldschmidt, A. (2005). *Als Freud das Meer sah*. Frankfurt am Main: Fischer.

Green, A. (1999). *The Work of the Negative*. London: Free Association Books.

Green, A. (2005). *Key Ideas for a Contemporary Psychoanalysis: Misrecognition and Recognition of the Unconscious*. London: Routledge.

Guex, G. (2015 [1951]). *The Abandonment Neurosis*. London: Karnac.

Joseph, B. (1997). *Psychic Equilibrium and Psychic Change*. London: Routledge.

Kohon, G. (1999). *No Lost Certainties to Be Recovered*. London: Karnac.

Kohon, G. (2016). *Reflections on the Aesthetic Experience*. London: Routledge.

Kohon, S. J. (2014). Making contact with the primitive mind: The contact barrier, beta-elements and the drives. *International Journal of Psychoanalysis, 95*:245–270.

Laub, D., & Lee, S. (2003). Thanatos and massive psychic trauma: The impact of the death instinct on knowing, remembering and forgetting. *Journal of the American Psychoanalytic Association, 51*:433–463.

M'Uzan, M. de, M. (2003). Identität und die Frage des Doppelgängers [Identity and the question of the double]. *Zeitschrift für psychoanalytische Theorie und Praxis*, *18*:88–102.

Parsons, M. (2016). *Psychic Freedom*. Unpublished conference presentation at the Vienna Psychoanalytic Society, June 10, 2016.

Pontalis, J. B. (1998). Über die Arbeit des Todes. In: *Zwischen Traum und Schmerz*. Frankfurt am Main: Fischer.

Reiter, B. (1996). Dunkel ist das Leben, ist der Tod: Zu Freuds Todestriebtheorie. *Zeitschrift für psychoanalytische Theorie und Praxis*, *11*:27–47.

Schnitzler, A. (1970 [1895]). *Dying*. Translated by A. Bell. London: Pushkin Press.

Segal, H. (1993). On the clinical usefulness of the concept of death instinct. *International Journal of Psychoanalysis*, *74*:55–61.

Zwettler-Otte, S. (2011a). *The Melody of Separation: A Psychoanalytic Study of Separation Anxiety*. Frankfurt am Main: Peter Lang.

Zwettler-Otte, S. (2011b). *Ebbe und Flut – Gezeiten des Eros. Psychoanalytische Gedanken und Fallstudien über die Liebe*. Stuttgart: Kohlhammer.

Zwettler-Otte, S. (2014). Fehl-Leistungen als Phänomene in psychoanalytischen Institutionen: "Das Unbehagen in der Kultur" wiedergelesen. *Jahrbuch der Psychoanalyse*, *69*:121–156.

CHAPTER 5

Is the concept of death drive clinically helpful for psychoanalysts?

Fritz Lackinger

A quote by Sigmund Freud in 1938 shows that the founder of psychoanalysis struggled with resistances to treatment related to the death drive until the bitter end of his life:

> There are some neurotics in whom, to judge by all their reactions, the instinct of self-preservation has actually been reversed. They seem to aim at nothing other than self-injury and self-destruction. It is possible too that the people who in fact do in the end commit suicide belong to this group. It is to be assumed that in such people far-reaching defusions of instinct [Triebentmischungen] have taken place, as a result of which there has been a liberation of excessive quantities of the destructive instinct directed inwards. Patients of this kind *are not able to tolerate recovery through our treatment and fight against it with all their strength*. But we must confess that this is a case which we have not yet succeeded in completely explaining.
>
> (Freud, 1940, p. 180, italics by the author)

Freud (1920) evidently introduced the concept of death drive into psychoanalytic metapsychology to a great extent for clinical reasons. As phenomena that contributed to the development of this concept we can mention:

1   The repetition compulsion, as a tendency both in treatment and in everyday life of many patients to the effect that traumatic or otherwise aversive experiences tend to restage themselves unconsciously time and again.

2   The syndromes of sadism and masochism; particularly the enjoyment of pain and humiliation seems to contradict the basic assumption of the pleasure principle that living matter in general seeks to avoid unpleasure.

3   The negative therapeutic reaction, as a clinical experience consisting in symptom deterioration as a consequence of helpful therapeutic interventions by the analyst.

4   Suicide, both in cases of major depression and in cases of severe character disorders without depression, as an obvious contradiction to the power of the instinct of self-preservation and as an indication of an utmost repulsion of any analytic help and support.

5   Destructive and self-destructive behaviour in large groups, as they bring to the fore drive derivatives that are normally repressed or at least suppressed, and thus demonstrate the existence of mighty forces that seem hardly compatible with the libidinal and self-preservation drive duality.

Freud (1940) does not situate the death drive exclusively in one of the fundamental structures of the psychic apparatus, although the super-ego seems to be one of its major locations from where it engenders its dangerous effects:

> When the super-ego is established, considerable amounts of the aggressive instinct are fixated in the interior of the ego and operate there self-destructively. This is one of the dangers to health by which human beings are faced on their path to cultural development. Holding back aggressiveness is in general unhealthy and leads to illness (to mortification). A person in a fit of rage will often demonstrate how the transition from aggressiveness that has been prevented to self-destructiveness is brought about by diverting the aggressiveness against himself: he tears his hair or beats his face with his fists, though he would evidently have preferred to apply this treatment to someone else. Some portion of self-destructiveness remains within, whatever the circumstances; till at last it succeeds in killing the individual, not, perhaps, until his libido has been used up or fixated in a disadvantageous way.
>
> (p. 150)

Also today we see very powerful clinical and political tendencies to self-destructiveness. The movements that strive to destroy the European unification process for example seem to attack not only the humanitarian and democratic achievements of the European project but to undermine arbitrarily the economic basis of European welfare and social stability. With Freud (1940, see preceding quote) we could formulate that parts of the population are not able to tolerate the achievements and rich possibilities of the European project and need to fight against it with all their strength. The insatiability of (self-)destructive forces shows itself even more in the acts of suicide terrorists who liquidate their own lives all too frequently together with many innocent others.

In the same sense, we face self-defeating and self-destructive behaviour in many psychopathological conditions that we have to deal with in psychoanalytical clinical practice: self-harm and even self-mutilation in borderline conditions; eating disorders that threaten health and even life of the patients; alcohol and drug addictions, sometimes with the potential of long-term harm and death; unsafe sexual promiscuity and other high-risk behaviour in the context of pathological sensation seeking; different forms of criminality devastating the lives of both victims and perpetrators. All these clinical phenomena confront us with challenging clinical tasks and often make us feeling helpless.

Freud (1940) admitted that he did not completely succeed in explaining the self-destructive phenomena that he encountered in his clinical work. He was sure that the death drive theory was an essential element of such an explanation, but how this drive translates and transforms itself into behavioural and transference phenomena was a different question. And so – in search of conceptual tools for orientating ourselves in situations of seemingly uncontrollable (self-)destructiveness – it may be of value to focus on some later developments of the concept, each of which is linked with different elements of Freud's thinking.

History

Historically, there have been several clinical approaches to further develop the psychoanalytic understanding of self-destructiveness. One should begin with Karl Abraham's attempt to re-visit the developmental stages of libido (Abraham, 1924), whereby he complemented Freud's anal-sadistic phase with an oral-sadistic phase at the end of the first year of life. The concept of oral sadism became very important for the understanding of depression and was related (although implicitly) to the death drive as developed by Melanie Klein (1932). Klein used the concept of the death drive to better understand the primitive anxieties of children as well as inform her strategy of interpreting the splitting and projecting of the aggressive and sadistic aspects of the self (Klein, 1946).

Along the same lines, we find Herbert Rosenfeld's thinking about the destructive aspects of narcissism from the 1960s onwards (1964, p. 1971). The concept of narcissism was introduced by Freud (1914) in the context of his first topographical model as an expression of the libidinal cathexis of the ego. Rosenfeld transposed the concept of narcissism onto the final Freudian drive model of Eros and Thanatos. For Rosenfeld, the self is not only associated with libidinal drive representations but also with destructive ones.

Other authors of the Kleinian tradition took up this question, e.g. Betty Joseph in the 1980s, Hanna Segal in the 1990s, and Michael Feldman early in this century (Joseph, 1982; Segal, 1997; Feldman, 2000). At the centre of these reflections lies the idea of an envious and hateful force that works to make the work of the analyst impossible, destroys his capacity to think, destroys the memory of analytic insights, and reverses the helpful analytic relationship into something harmful and damaging.

Betty Joseph (1982) especially pointed to a state that she called "addiction to near-death." She found that certain patients present a masochistic and sexually arousing fixation onto states of hopelessness and despair. Although they do not seek physical death, they permanently seek deep states of anxiety and depressive feelings for masochistic reasons. Betty Joseph emphasizes that the analyst should find a way to differentiate between authentic feelings of guilt and despair, on the one hand, and their instrumentalization in the service of a perversion that takes the form of an addiction to near-death, on the other hand. These patients find it difficult to recognize the satisfaction they experience from their chronic induction of hopelessness, and even more difficult to endure and tolerate authentic pain.

But there is also a non-Kleinian tradition that makes clinical use of the death drive model. I only mention André Green (1983, 1999, 2001) who developed the concepts of negative narcissism and disobjectalization as applications of this concept. Green pointed to the fact that it was Freud's late considerations about the death drive that allowed the psychoanalytic technique to expand its application from the neuroses to more severe character pathologies (Green, 2001). Object-related aggression has to be differentiated from disobjectalizing destruction. Green proposes the idea that the essential goal of life drives (Eros) is to guarantee an objectifying function by cathecting objects with drive energy thus promoting an object relationship. In contrast, the essential goal of the death drives is to ensure a disobjectalizing function through unbinding.

Fundamental importance

The death drive concept stands up against the prevalent and more optimistic view of human nature according to which chronic frustration and childhood trauma leads to human aggression. Sigmund Freud himself was convinced of the necessity of a measure of pessimism leads to scientific and psychoanalytic world view.

> If I doubt man's destiny to climb by way of civilisation to a state of greater perfection, if I see in life a continual struggle between Eros and the death instinct, the outcome of which seems to me to be indeterminable, I do not believe that in coming to those conclusions I have been influenced by innate constitutional factors or acquired emotional attitudes. I am neither a self-tormentor nor am I cussed and, if I could, I should gladly do as others do and bestow upon mankind a rosy future, and I should find it much more beautiful and consoling if we could count on such a thing. But this seems to me to be yet another instance of illusion (wish fulfilment) in conflict with truth. The question is not what belief is more pleasing or more comfortable or more advantageous to life, but of what may approximate more closely to the puzzling reality that lies outside us. The death instinct is not a requirement of my heart; it seems to me to be only an inevitable assumption on both biological and psychological grounds. The rest follows from that. Thus to me my pessimism seems a conclusion, while the optimism of my opponents seems an *a priori* assumption.
>
> (Meng & Freud, 1963, letter from Sigmund Freud to
> Oskar Pfister, February 7, 1930, pp. 132–133)

Freud admits that the pure death drive is a speculative postulate that never can be directly observed. Clinically, we find the death drive always fused with the life drive. But this must not allow us to underestimate the destructive quality of some of these partial drive fusions, especially as they are liable to become defused again as Freud explains in relation to the sadistic perversion:

> Once we have admitted the idea of a fusion of the two classes of instincts with each other, the possibility of a – more or less complete – "defusion" of them forces itself upon us. The sadistic component of the sexual instinct would be a classical example of a serviceable instinctual fusion; and the sadism which has made itself independent as a perversion would be typical of a defusion, though not of one carried to extremes . . . we come to understand that instinctual defusion and the marked emergence of the death instinct call for particular consideration among the effects of some severe neuroses.
>
> (Freud, 1923, pp. 41–42)

Psychoanalysts with a basically neurotic personality structure tend to underestimate the abysses of human nature as we are used to repress our outright destructive wishes and impulses into the unconscious. We are usually able to stably repress them because our psychic apparatus has developed the necessary strength to do so. But as is well known from psychological experiments and the history of mass violence, large quotas of the so-called normal population are able to take part in unbelievable atrocities.

Our more severely disturbed patients are not able to repress their destructive tendencies in the same way as normal and neurotic people. At the same time the nature of their psychic organization leads to strong tendencies of both projecting and re-introjecting their destructive impulses. Therefore, we encounter self-destructiveness as a typical feature of the transference process in many borderline and narcissistic patients. But these tendencies often are disguised and we are not immediately able to recognize them. Importantly, our own resistances may contribute to a misinterpretation that considers an obstruction of the analytic process as resulting from archaic anxieties and overlooks the satisfaction that is drawn from self-destruction.

For this reason, Freud's concept of the death drive is clinically necessary: it posits destructivity at the centre of our model of the mind, as one of the two basic motivations of the human being. It reminds us to never underestimate the force of our destructive and self-destructive drives and to accept that self-destructiveness is not simply the reflection of guilt and anxiety deterring the patient from life success and erotic satisfaction, but that it is a wish finding expression in feelings of triumphant superiority or perverted lust.

Examples

I want to illustrate my understanding of the death drive's relevance for our clinical practice with three examples. One is a severely masochistic patient which could not be treated successfully. The other is a patient that Betty Joseph presented to make clear some important features of an addiction to near-death. The third case is a less dramatic example of the effect of death drive–related unconscious guilt that I have found in an analysis with a complicated hysteric woman.

Mrs M

This patient came to me after her sixth psychiatric hospitalization due to a drug overdose. She regularly committed self-injury by heavily beating her forearms against the edge of a table until they were completely blue and had to be covered for several days. She was bulimic, with initially daily, later weekly, bouts, until she could give up this symptom early during treatment. She suffered from mood swings and several anxieties, especially related to exams. Frequently she felt tired and exhausted and unable to learn. She had only few social contacts, which she tended to neglect. And she was desperately intimately bound to her parents, both personally and financially, to the extent that she never dared to contradict them or even to tell them about her problems or that she was in therapy.

In the first year of therapy she struggled with the few remaining exams of her teacher training course, seemingly unable to learn and memorize the course material. She always failed in the first trial and seemed to pass the exams the second time by luck only. After ten years of study she finally completed the teacher training for religion and mathematics. She began to teach the lower classes of a general secondary school, but she remained completely isolated from her colleagues because she felt easily attacked and retreated preventively before any actual attack could take place.

During these months it became clear that Mrs M regularly came into a critical state whenever an exam date was approaching. During these periods the probability of self-injury increased. The first time the patient came with covered forearms into the analytic session we agreed she would see her primary physician whenever she self-mutilated herself, and let the wounds be cared for. I told her that as her psychoanalyst I didn't want to be responsible for her wound management, but at the same time I needed to be sure that her wounds were cared for properly so that no secondary complications would arise. Although she was unhappy with my demand she agreed, but from that moment on she switched to drug overdoses as her preferred form of self-harm. She abused the medication of her psychiatrist who had prescribed quetiapine to help her control her self-harming impulses. In other words, she used something that was meant to help to self-harm herself instead. Usually on Friday evenings she took up to 2000 mg, then opened the door of her flat and phoned the ambulance. She was found unconscious on the floor and taken to the hospital, where she awoke the day following. She had a great routine in convincing the psychiatrists on-duty that she was in control of her suicidality and they let her go home one day later. On the following Monday she went to work as if nothing had happened. She adopted the same attitude at her Monday session: as if nothing had happened and if therapy simply could go on.

When I confronted her with the fact that her behaviour represented an aggression against therapy she smiled for a moment and then said I had forbidden her to hit her arms against her table and so she had no choice but to overdose her drugs. She managed to make me responsible for her para-suicidal act and in this way again, she reversed something positive and helpful, namely, my demand for her to care for her wounds, into something destructive. Such distortions were typical for this patient. They were symptomatic not so much of a sexual perversion, which she probably had as well, but a characterological perversity. Otto Kernberg (1992) defined perversity as eroticism and love put into the service of aggression, as something good being transformed into something bad, love into hate, cooperation into exploitation, nurture into defecation, etc.

Patient A

The following case example is taken from the contribution of Betty Joseph (1982) on addiction to near-death. At the start of the analysis with Betty Joseph, A was cold, almost cruel, but during the course of the treatment he became more warm-hearted. Monday had been a good session in which a hidden way of him being cruel and provocative had been jointly explored. Tuesday, he overslept the session and Wednesday he presented his surprise, that after the good Monday session and the feeling of relief at the end of the session he had felt disastrously bad during the night.

He seemed perplexed about his sleeplessness and his missing of the Tuesday session. He said that possibly he was stuck too deep in this horrible state so that he could not be helped out of it at all. This had already been the theme of the Monday session.

Then he recounted a dream: he found himself in a long, rather big cave which was dark and smoky. He felt that he and other people had been captured by a gang of robbers. It seemed that there was quite a mess and a confusion, as if they were drunken. The robbers stood in a row along a wall, and he (the dreamer) sat next to a young man who looked friendly, was in his mid-20s, and had a small moustache. Suddenly the man turned to him and grapped him, reaching for his genitals, as if the man was homosexual. The dreamer felt panic as the man was about to stab him with a knife.

As an association to the dream, the patient remembered that a business friend had told him that a colleague of his was very much afraid of the patient. This colleague scared the patient so much that he trembled physically when phoning him. The patient associated this story with a remark of the analyst about his "cold manner", with which he had treated her after she had doubted something he had said. Then the patient spoke again about the young friendly man of the dream who turned out to be so cruel. The moustache was associated with the poet DH Lawrence who is said to have been both homosexual and violent.

The cave stood for the place wherein he felt inescapably and chronically pulled into and where he felt stuck too deep to be helped out of it. It was a central element of an unconscious masochistic transference phantasy that fitted well with the fascination (in the dream) that the robbers had triggered in the patient. The robbers represented sadistic inner objects, with whom a part of the patient had identified while the other part of his personality submitted masochistically to them. The surrender to the dream-robbers had apparently turned out to be sexually arousing.

Joseph draws the consequence that the despair and its description during the session came along with a real masochistic and self-destructive arousal. The patient spoke as if trying to draw the analyst into his misery (and let him concordantly experience masochistic pain), or as if he wanted to provoke the analyst to disturbing comments (thus making him an accomplice of the robber-part-self).

Mrs C

The following clinical material is from a patient who suffered from long-standing anxieties about being afflicted by epileptic seizures. Although neurological examinations clearly spoke against any epileptic disposition, both the patient and her whole family held on to this diagnosis. She was convinced that only anti-epileptic medication could save her from regular seizures. As she nevertheless developed what she called "absences," she began to take benzodiazepines in addition to calm her fears. She was preoccupied with fears and drugs and this restricted her possibilities to live a satisfying life. She felt locked-in into a feeling of being ill.

What I summarize here in a few lines emerged over five years of psychoanalysis. For years she hid her chronic abuse and low-dose-addiction to benzodiazepines. But finally we could explore the different states she mistook as epileptic gradually realising they were psychologically motivated dissociated states. She tried to avoid situations of rivalry and envy by producing so-called absences or – in her puberty – hysteric seizures. But that insight did not in and of itself lead to improvement. She remained anxious, preoccupied, and addicted to drugs.

I agreed with the patient that she should see a psychiatrist to discuss her abuse of tranquilizers and anti-epileptic drugs as she clearly did not need either of them. But, in fact, for a long time she did not contact a psychiatrist, and when she finally did, she did not manage to get an appointment. Nothing happened. As with many other intentions the patient did not take any decisive step to realize the plan.

The resistance to take advantage of her insights was obvious and I began to interpret them as self-harming. She immediately accepted this perspective and said she became anxious as soon as she really began to fight against withdrawal and addiction. She had the feeling she did not deserve any fundamental change to the better. Her unconscious conviction was that she had to stay ill.

Analytic work brought to light that when she was two and a half years old a younger brother died after he was diagnosed as an epileptic. It turned out that my patient had felt guilty both for the death of the one-year-old boy and for the consecutive depression of the mother. But again, these insights helped only temporarily. A deadly stagnation came back again and hopelessness seemed to prevail. This was reflected in a countertransferential reaction in the analyst who felt anger against the apparent non-absorption of the preceding process of interpretation by the patient. Reflection about this feeling made it possible to not impulsively interpret the patient's sealing off in a defensive manner.

It was necessary to understand how the feeling of guilt had not been accepted by the patient as a child, and how she instead identified with the necessity to punish herself for her crimes. An unconscious part was deeply convinced that she deserved a lifelong punishment for killing her brother, and for making her mother so unhappy. This part of herself demanded her to stay ill for her whole life and found a specific unconscious excitation and satisfaction in destroying her liveliness. Any attempt to break free from her chronic self-harming unleashed an angry attack from the side of that retaliating masochistic part.

Technical implications

The case vignettes illustrate the unconscious working of a drive that neither follows the pleasure principle nor can its appearance as a superego-type punishment be understood alone as a prohibitive counter-cathexis against repressed libidinal drive wishes. The superego in these cases is rather a manifestation of a drive to self-harm and self-destruction in and of itself. Superego moralism – the feeling to deserve pain, harm, and death – is used primarily as a rationalization of self-destructiveness whereas the repression of any erotic zest for life and the prevention of any libidinal satisfaction serves the aim of self-harm directly or is secondarily hijacked by the unconscious strategy of the death drive.

Based on the works of Freud (1914, 1920, 1923, 1940), Abraham (1924), Klein (1932, 1946), Rosenfeld (1964, 1971), Joseph (1982), Segal, (1997) Green (1983, 1999, 2001), Feldman (2000), and Kernberg (1992, 2009) it is possible to draw important technical conclusions from clinical experience with cases where self-destructiveness is a prominent motivational factor. I can give only a quite condensed summary here:

- Diagnostical alertness is important, as (self-)destructive tendencies frequently hide behind uneventfulness and boredom. (Self-)destructive behaviour is not necessarily spontaneously reported in the initial interview. Thus we actively have to search for hints in this respect and explore these thoroughly.
- As much as possible, self-destructive tendencies have to be detected and analysed from the beginning, especially insofar as they manifest themselves in the transference, for example, as a tendency to destroy everything that comes from the analyst (which does not exclude a parallel hope that the analyst might survive the aggression of the patient).
- If the acting out of the patient is potentially capable of destroying the therapeutic setting (e.g. by suicidality, excessive drug abuse, violent offending, or anorectic weight loss), a structuring of the treatment by means of a treatment contract might be necessary. This is because any analysis of (self-)destructiveness becomes impossible if the treatment is discontinued.
- Patients who are incapable of controlling their (self-)destructive acting out (which may e.g. be seen from a treatment record that includes several broken therapy processes) should perhaps not be seen in a high-frequency couch setting as this tends to reinforce their regression and their dangerous irresponsibility in terms of the therapy agreements.
- The (usually verbal) contract in these cases has to state the potential dangers to the therapy setting and a way of dealing with them that does protects the therapy. It has also to be clarified in advance which consequences any break of such agreements has. Borderline patients often provocatively play with agreements and therefore need to know the contracted limits to their (playful?) provocations.
- During therapy, deviations from technical neutrality can be necessary to save the life of the patient or the therapy itself. But such deviations need to be interpreted subsequently as consequences of a

hostile transference acting out resulting from the patient being identified with or under the control of a sadistic internalized part object.
The aim of such interpretations is the earliest possible reinstatement
of technical neutrality.

- Patients who have (self-)destructive tendencies but do not impulsively enact them can and should be seen in a high-frequency couch
setting, especially if their character pathology is of a higher level
quality. Many depressive, schizoid, and even narcissistic personalities can successfully be analysed in the classic setting.

- Self-destructive patients commonly show signs of severe suffering;
however, their suffering frequently does not evoke genuine compas-
sion in the analyst. Such a lack of sympathy can arouse feelings of bad
faith in the analyst although it may be a reflection of the patients instrumentalization of suffering in the service of (self-)destructiveness. It is
very important to elaborate with the patient the difference between
authentic pain and anxiety as opposed to the use of pain, anxiety, and
hopelessness for masochistic reasons.

- It is equally important to analyse the satisfaction that is created by
the aggression of the patient against himself and against others.
Sometimes we see triumphant delight, which is quite disturbing for
the analyst, and in perverse transference situations it can also be
sexual lust that is activated by masochistic self-destruction. It is not
uncommon that such delight and pleasure is only reluctantly and
grudgingly recognized by the patient.

- Psychopathic transferences show themselves in systematic dishon-
esty of the patient vis-à-vis the analyst. This may also transpire during the analysis of many less disturbed narcissistic personalities. It
reflects a deep mistrust of the analyst and has as aim to disrupt his
ambitions by preventing any fair-minded analytic relationship. By
interpretation of the insincerity as a preventive action against being
cheated and deceived by the analyst, the psychopathic transference
can often be overcome.

- Psychopathic and perverse transferences usually transform themselves into paranoid transferences before giving way to higher levels
of integration. The reason for this lies in the fact that the psychopathic
and perverse patient tries to avoid his deep-seated anxieties vis-à-vis
the analyst by way of deception and manipulation. To make these
anxieties conscious leads to paranoid transference, which however
has to be seen as a progress in treatment.

- In cases of long-lasting stagnation in analytic treatments one needs to be particularly vigilant, since they may be the result of a deadly repetition compulsion which is used to avoid vital conflicts and deny the passing of time. The denial of the importance of time in analysis and in life in general is a frequent symptom of narcissistic escapism ostensibly in the service of the pleasure principle but really in the service of self-hatred and self-destruction.

References

Abraham, K. (1924). A short study of the development of the libido. In: R. V. Frankiel (Ed.), *Essential Papers on Object Loss* (pp. 73–93). New York: New York University Press, 1994.

Feldman, M. (2000). Some views on the manifestation of the death instinct in clinical work. *International Journal of Psychoanalysis*, *81*:53–65.

Freud, S. (1914). *On Narcissism: An Introduction*. Standard Edition 14:67–102.

Freud, S. (1920). *Beyond the Pleasure Principle*. Standard Edition 18:1–64.

Freud, S. (1923). *The Ego and the Id*. Standard Edition 19:1–66.

Freud, S. (1940 [1938]). *An Outline of Psycho-Analysis*. Standard Edition 23:139–208.

Green, A. (1983). *Narcissisme de vie, Narcissisme de mort*. Paris: Minuit.

Green, A. (1999). The death drive, negative narcissism and the disobjectalising function. In: A. Green (Ed.), *The Work of the Negative*. Translated by A. Weller (pp. 81–88). London: Free Association Books.

Green, A. (2001). *Life Narcissism, Death Narcissism*. London: Free Association Books.

Joseph, B. (1982). Addiction to near-death. *International Journal of Psychoanalysis*, *63*:449–456.

Kernberg, O. F. (1992). *Aggression in Personality Disorders and Perversions*. New Haven, CT: Yale University Press.

Kernberg, O. F. (2009). The concept of the death drive: A clinical perspective. *International Journal of Psychoanalysis*, *90*:1009–1023.

Klein, M. (1932). *The Psycho-Analysis of Children*. New Edition. London: Vintage, 1997.

Klein, M. (1946). Notes on some schizoid mechanisms. In: M. M. Khan (Ed.), *Envy and Gratitude and Other Works 1946–1963* (pp. 1–24). London: Hogart, 1975.

Meng, H., & Freud, E. L. (1963). Psychoanalysis and faith: The letters of Sigmund Freud and Oskar Pfister. *International Psycho-Analytic Library*, 59:1–147. London: Hogarth.

Rosenfeld, H. (1964). On the psychopathology of narcissism: A clinical approach. *International Journal of Psychoanalysis*, 45:332–337. Republished in: H. Rosenfeld (Ed.), *Psychotic States: A Psychoanalytic Approach* (pp. 169–179). London: Hogarth, 1965.

Rosenfeld, H. (1971). A clinical approach to the psychoanalytic theory of the life and death instincts: An investigation into the aggressive aspects of narcissism. *International Journal of Psychoanalysis*, 52:169–178. Republished in: E. Bott Spillius (Ed.), *Melanie Klein Today, Volume 1* (pp. 239–255). London: Routledge, 1988.

Segal, H. (1993). On the clinical usefulness of the concept of the death instinct. *International Journal of Psychoanalysis*, 74:55–61. Republished in: J. Steiner (Ed.), *Psychoanalysis, Literature and War: Papers 1972–1995* (pp. 17–26). London: Routledge, 1997.

PART III
CULTURE

CHAPTER 6

Vicissitudes of the death drive in culture

Elisabeth Skale

In his paper "Instincts and Their Vicissitudes," Freud defines drives as a "measure of the demand for work (*Arbeitsanforderung*) made upon the mind in consequence of its connection with the body" (Freud, 1915, p. 122). Experienced as needs which cannot be fled, drives can only be satisfied through changes applied to their source in order to avoid unpleasurable feelings. Faced with the pressure of the drives, the mental apparatus has to renounce its ideal intention of keeping off stimuli and to tolerate a certain amount of constant stimulation. In order to regulate the stimulation coming from the drives,[1] the apparatus has to find modes of defence, which Freud describes as their different vicissitudes in the process of development and in the course of life: (1) reversal into its opposite, (2) turning around upon the subject's own self, (3) repression, and (4) sublimation.

In order to illustrate the different vicissitudes of the sexual drive, Freud examines two pairs of opposites: sadism-masochism and scopophilia-exhibitionism. In both cases, the turning around upon the subject's self converges or coincides with a transformation from activity to passivity, which in sadism-masochism is additionally accompanied by a reversal of content: love is transformed into hate and at the same time the object is changed while the aim remains the same (Freud, 1915,

p. 127). Freud explicitly restricts his description to the sexual drive – he does not include what was regarded as the antagonist of the sexual drive at that time, the self-preservative drives or "ego drives."

After his paper "Beyond the Pleasure Principle" (1920), Freud had to revise his drive theory to include the death drive as the antagonist of the "life drives." But he never explicitly addressed the issue of specific vicissitudes of the death drive. Moreover, with the newly introduced concept of fusion and defusion of the drives and their interplay and interaction (as described for the first time in 1923 in "The Ego and the Id"), Freud relinquished the idea of following the vicissitudes of just one drive alone. He now explained the processes of "reversal into its opposite" and "turning against the subject's own self," by the more complex and seminal concept of the mutual influence, or mixture of both drives. Originally, their orientation is opposite to each other, with the sexual drive being directed outwards and the death drive being oriented inwards. For the vicissitudes of repression and sublimation, too, the characteristics of the antagonistic drives – the cathecting, binding, and fusing capacity of the sexual drive and the unbinding, decathecting, and defusing tendency of the death drive – play an important role.

The fusion of drives leads to an interplay of their functioning. According to Freud,

> the modifications in the proportions of the fusion between the instincts have the most tangible results. A surplus of sexual aggressiveness will turn a lover into a sex-murderer, while a sharp diminution in the aggressive factor will make him bashful or impotent.
>
> (Freud, 1940, p. 149)

When Freud speaks about the defusion of drives, he often refers to the then unlimited aggressiveness as a manifestation of the death drive, which breaks all ties with sexuality. Nevertheless it still shows many characteristics of the sexual drive, and therefore remains a product of drive fusion. Rather than a manifestation of the "pure" death drive, which eludes our perception, "unless it is tinged with erotism" (Freud, 1930, p. 120). In "The Economic Problem of Masochism" (1924), Freud defined erotogenic masochism as a primary manifestation of the death drive and thus as one of its central clinical vicissitudes.

In this contribution, I compile some speculative ideas about certain cultural phenomena that seem to have been shaped by the fundamental qualities and characteristics of the death drive. In this way, they represent the vicissitudes of the death drive in culture and civilization.

The two faces of the death drive in Freud's "Beyond the Pleasure Principle"

If we wish to think about the manifestations of the death drive in culture, we have to take into account the specific characteristics of Freud's concept. In "Beyond the Pleasure Principle" he introduced the death drives as forces directed against the life drives, with the death drives striving to reduce tension to zero and therefore representing the tendency of a living being to return to an inorganic state. Barbara Low, to whom Freud refers, stated in 1920: "It is possible that deeper than the Pleasure-principle lies the Nirvana-principle, as one may call it – the desire of the newborn creature to return to that stage of omnipotence, where there are no non-fulfilled desires, in which it existed within the mother's womb" (Low, 1920, p. 72).

Freud characterized the death drive as directed inwards with a tendency towards disintegration, decathexis, reduction of tension, opposition to any movement, a state of standstill, and omnipotent self-dissolution. In these respects, the death drive is a direct antagonist of the sexual drive. At the same time, Freud thought that its regressive tendency and repetitive nature represent the very essence of a drive in general. The death drive, conceptualized as one of the "ego instincts," is directed towards the ego, while its antagonist, the sexual drive, as an "object instinct," is directed towards objects. In this sense, the death drive is present in the ego and is diverted by narcissistic libido from the ego onto objects of the outside world as the "instinct for mastery", as the "destructive instinct" and the "will to power", partly in the service of the sexual function as sadism. Masochism, the turning around of the destructive instinct upon the subject's ego, would then be a regression, a return to an earlier phase of the instinct's history. With the new idea of a death drive present in the ego, the idea of primary masochism (which Freud already speculated about in 1915, but contested it at that time) seemed to be confirmed.

Freud described two apparently contradictory characteristics of the death drive: first, the drive works silently to reduce tensions in order to annihilate life, and second, it is a force originally directed against the ego but then deflected onto external objects, where it becomes loud and causes tension and destruction.

This seeming contradiction could be resolved when we see aggression or the so-called destructive instinct as the first vicissitude of the death drive, as its passive aim – the dissolution of the ego – is turned into an activity against the outer world. This turnaround leads to a change of object and to a reversal of its quality according to Freud's definition of 1915.

This would help to clarify the distinction between the manifestation of the death drive proper and the various manifestations of its vicissitude as a "destructive instinct," with the latter having been explored extensively in clinical and social contexts.

Melanie Klein partly followed Freud in conceptualizing the death drive as a disintegrating force within the ego that causes the fear of annihilation of the ego (1932). But for Klein, the death drive is not only deflected from the ego onto the outside world, it is also projected into outer objects in order to protect the ego and to prevent self-destruction. The mechanisms of projection, introjection, and splitting serve from the beginning of life to help the ego to overcome anxiety and relieve it of danger and badness. Klein points out that although these objects are felt to be external, they become internal persecutors through introjection and thus reinforce the fear of the destructive impulse within (1946). With this, Klein defines the superego as a part of the ego that is initially separated as a container of the death drive and as rather hostile to the ego, until the introjection of loving parental objects mitigates its harshness.

Ronald Britton criticizes Klein's concept of an innate death drive underlying the ego's annihilation anxiety that only in a second step is turned into a destructive tendency against objects. He sees this as a detour she made by following Freud too closely and states that hostility towards objects on the outside is a primary drive, which he links to a basic "xenocidal impulse," an impulse to destroy the foreign, to annihilate anything other than the self. Britton, however, concedes that these "anti-object relational" forces can "act against any attachment to an object, including those within the mind – memories, desires, perceptions, thoughts, and so forth. In some extreme cases, it might result in attacks on the mental and perceptual apparatus itself" (2006, p. 4). With this interpretation, he comes close to the idea of a death drive that aims to dissolve any structures of the own ego (cf. Bell, 2015).

In this chapter, I would like to concentrate on the "silent" death drive, which has not been turned into aggressiveness but instead seeks to eliminate disturbances, and discuss some ideas about how it shows itself in the individual, in civilization, and in the arts.

Manifestations of the death drive in civilization: the conscience of society

When Freud speaks about the human "instinct of aggression and self-destruction" as the opposing drive to eternal Eros in "Civilization and Its Discontents" (1930), he never directly equates the aggressive instinct with the death drive. Rather, he attributes the "will to power" and "aggression" as phenomena of a destructive instinct deriving from the deflected death drive, and refers to regressive, dissolving, and unbinding tendencies as forces directly coming from the death drive.

With regard to civilizing processes, Freud describes several factors that are constitutional and specific to civilization but at the same time contribute to its discontent and unhappiness: "The taming of the instinctual libidinal forces by the reality-principle in society can be only achieved by repression or other defenses, which block the course towards satisfaction." Only the taming by sublimation – an artist's joy in creating or the scientist solving problems or discovering truths – provides at least some satisfaction, but its intensity "is mild as compared with that derived from the sating of crude and primary instinctual impulses; it does not convulse our physical being" (Freud, 1930, p. 79).

Besides the libidinal forces, Freud also has to deal with aggressive tendencies, and he finally postulates an "inborn human inclination to 'badness,' to aggressiveness and destructiveness, and so to cruelty" (Freud, 1930, p. 120). This natural aggressive instinct, a hostility against each other as expressed in "homo homini lupus," opposes the program of civilization and poses the threat of disintegration to civilized society (Freud, 1930, p. 111).

Freud connects the individual's and society's development in the process of taming "inborn" aggressiveness. The individual's "aggressiveness is introjected, internalized, it is taken over by a portion of the ego, which sets itself over against the rest of the ego as super-ego" (Freud, 1930, p. 123). The superego is ready to act against the ego with the same harsh aggressiveness that the ego would have liked to inflict upon its objects. The process of civilization is aimed at obtaining "mastery over the individual's dangerous desire for aggression by weakening and disarming it and by setting up an agency within him to watch over it, like a garrison in a conquered city" (Freud, 1930, p. 234).

This process of the development of a superego in the individual can be also found in society when governmental structures are implemented. In both instances, the process itself shows characteristics of the workings of the death drive; it is a force directed against the ego, orientated inwards, which precipitates as a structure heading for a "standstill": a superego inside a subject or a legislative or executive body within society which controls and regulates aggressive and libidinal wishes. The forces precipitate as a structure that becomes the harsher the higher the level of aggression in the individual or in society. The relation between ego and superego shows different dynamics: a harsh, immature, or impaired (sadistic) superego aims to force the ego into submission, an endeavour that is sometimes met by a passive, masochistic tendency of the ego. Or the ego identifies with the prohibitive force of the superego and turns it against itself reflexively, as a self-punishing attitude, like in the obsessional neurosis in the individual. Alternatively, the ego may also be able to identify with a mitigated superego and may even gain strength and orientation from it. Which one of these dynamics comes into effect depends on the fusion or defusion of the life drive and the death drive, especially on the scope of death drive derivatives, which serve as stabilizing structures.

The democratic division of power, protected by a system of checks and balances, serves as the superego of the state that produces and executes the law but is at the same time subject to constitutional law itself. Analogous to the situation in individuals, any such social structure can also be turned into a dictatorship in the sense of a suppressing and destructive superego, when the death drive derivatives become too strong. In order to distinguish different levels of influence of the death drive, we have to differentiate openly undemocratic, autocratic, or dictatorial governmental structures, as manifestations of an extremely harsh and unjust "social superego," from the effects of the excess of the "silent" death drive that aims to undermine and dissolve any structure. In clinical terms, the "undermining" superego is encountered in the psychopathic personality. At the societal level', we are currently witnessing how in Europe "antidemocratic" processes have been set in motion, whereby political and often populist movements oppose or undermine democratic structures in a secret and seductive manner. These phenomena can be attributed to an unbalanced effect of death drive tendencies. Parliaments and other constitutional (superego) structures of the state are attacked as overly restrictive and invasive, and people believe in the promise that they will be "freed" from them. These movements aim to erode and ultimately dissolve the state's self-imposed control structures and replace them with dictatorial and unpredictable ones.

The processes outlined here reveal the two different effects of the death drive as an antagonist of the sexual drive: when fused with the sexual drive and turned inward, the death drive's striving for a standstill and its "silencing" tendencies are mitigated, and they manifest themselves as confinements of the sexual drive's activity. In this sense, a stabilizing and "constructive" tendency can be attributed to the death drive, insofar as it helps build up structures like the superego that which then take on the task of the continuous control of the activities of the sexual drive. Similarly, in Cordelia Schmidt-Hellerau's model of psychoanalytic drive and structure theory, the death drive is conceptualized as a force against the life drives and vice versa. The drives set boundaries for each other and serve as each other's repression. "Psychic structure arises at the precise time and place where a drive tendency switches over into a repression tendency", hence structure can be described as a "drive-repression unity" (Schmidt-Hellerau, 1995, p. 107).

In this sense, the conservative nature of the death drive seems to be also in the service of the reality principle, by taming, silencing, and structuring "loud" aggression, as a product of the fusion with the life drives. Only when a defusion of the drives leads to an excess of the death drive does the latter unimpededly strive towards dissolution and decathecting of both life and structures as a manifestation of its inherent "silent" destructivity. Therefore, as mentioned previously, describing aggression as a direct manifestation of the death drive may be quite seductive, but would actually impoverish the idea and concept of the death drive as it would deny the dissolving and tension-reducing qualities as well as its conservative and stabilizing nature.

"Perversion" of the death drive in the individual and in society

The idealization of an instinct, like Freud described it in the context of a perversion of the sexual instinct in "Three Essays on the Theory of Sexuality," is in fact the opposite of a defence in neurotic terms. Nevertheless, it can be seen as a vicissitude of an instinct. The mental work involved in perversions to make the polymorphic aims of the instinct egosyntonic is "equivalent to an idealization of the instinct." The former polymorphic deities, says Freud, which are turned into demons defensively, have to undergo a secondary deification to survive (Freud, 1905, p. 161).

A perversion of the death drive can be seen as an idealization of its aims: reducing "life tension" and retreating from the outer world by decathecting internal and external relationships. These processes can undermine or dissolve ego structures as well as superego structures in the individual and they can suspend social connections by heading towards "unconsciousness," which Ernst Simmel defined as complete instinct repose:

> This condition of absolute unconsciousness may be considered the mental equivalent of physical death. Freud believed the immanent striving of our mental system towards release of tension is characteristic of the operation of a death instinct (the Nirvana principle of Barbara Low) – a struggle which comes to expression in the pleasure principle – and is indeed one of our strongest motives for believing in the existence of death instincts.
>
> (1944, p. 175)

But as André Green pointed out, two opposing nuances can be found in the Nirvana state:

> On the one hand it was conceived as an active self-destruction which led to fragmentation, to chaos, and finally to Nothing, considered as a sort of demoniac unfolding of instinctual energy, on the other hand, this Nothing could be conceived of as the terminal phase of a wish for repose and peace, like a search – destructive or not – for non-stimulation, for the fading of all obstacles to homeostasis.
>
> (Folch & de Folch, 1984)

Green states that already in 1914, when introducing the concept of narcissism, Freud had defended "the idea of an internal destructivity in the form of a self-sufficiency which denies the object's existence" and that "[t]his destructive modality is quite different from aggressivity directed outwards or turned back against the ego" (Green, 1999, p. 105). André Green's concept of "negative narcissism" (1999) is not only an expression of a disobjectalizing function focusing on objects and their substitutes but on the very process of objectalizing itself. Similarly, in connection to certain clinical manifestations like infantile apathy and anaclitic depression, Ikonen and Rechardt describe a "black narcissism," a striving for undisturbed emptiness, which "seeks to remove and extinguish both the narcissistic and the object-directed, unsatisfied, unbound and disturbing libido" and attribute it to the death drive (Ikonen & Rechardt, 1978, p. 102, footnote).

Regression, as a psychic mechanism, and even the wish to sleep have characteristics of a death drive activity and seem to be in the service of the death drive "as a return to an earlier, simpler state, which is better under control, precedes the disturbance and contains less of it" (Ikonen & Rechardt, 1978, p. 104). In this sense, the hypothetical perversion of the death drive is the idealization of a regressive, objectless, and lifeless state. It is well known that a similar striving can be observed in substance-related addictions. Besides the direct drug effect of making people feel tranquil and euphoric, thus easing psychic pain and disturbing experiences, it is the transgression and dissolution of boundaries which is praised and craved. But also in non-substance-related addictions, in games, videogames, and other internet activities, mindlessness seems to be a prominent goal. Addictive sexual voyeurism under virtual conditions has the characteristics of a perversion of the death drive, of being drawn into a mindless state and retreating from reality. I think it will be an important topic for further discussion whether virtual reality and the "darknet" can be seen as spheres of action for a drive characterized by its silence, its inward pull, by its tendency to dissolve bonds and to undermine structures.

A perversion of the death drive can be also found in a completely different field. By coming back to civilization and legal processes, I would like to point to the legal practice of the death penalty as a manifestation of the death drive in disguise of a legal process. Judith Butler refers to Jacques Derrida's viewpoints on the death penalty in her lecture "Politics of the Death Drive: The Case of the Death Penalty." She writes: "When the state kills, and justifies doing so, it enacts vengeance through its reasoning process; legal violence becomes no different from non-legal violence, except that now the state performs the act and supplies its justification" (Butler, 2014).

The violence involved in the act of the death penalty is not the destructive act of enforcing the death penalty per se but the process of legally justifying it. The act of justification is an idealization of a defused death drive, a perversion of it characterized by its silent deadliness.

Sublimation and the struggle for
representation of the death drive in culture

Interestingly, Freud never wrote a paper on sublimation even though he announced he would do so already in 1915, and he never explicitly considered a sublimation of the death drive. Still, he addressed the problem of sublimation of the "destructive instinct" in one of his letters to Marie Bonaparte, dated May 27, 1937. He underscored that the instinct of destruction can be sublimated by being directed towards another, socially more acceptable goal:

> All activities that rearrange or effect changes are to a certain extent destructive and thus redirect a portion of the instinct from its original destructive goal. Even the sexual instinct, as we know, cannot act without some measure of aggression. Therefore in the regular combination of the two instincts there is a partial sublimation of the destructive instinct. One may regard finally curiosity, the impulse to investigate, as a complete sublimation of the aggressive or destructive instinct. Altogether in the life of the intellect the instinct attains a high significance as the motor of all discrimination, denial and condemnation.
>
> (Jones, 1957, p. 494)

Freud's statement about the sublimation of the "destructive instinct" and its relevance for intellectual work is highly valuable also for thinking about cultural production and its consumption as an interplay between binding and releasing forces in the struggle for the representation of the death drive in culture.

Hanns Sachs and later Hannah Segal wrote about the role the death drive plays for the production of art and the aesthetic experience. In his paper of 1940, Sachs looks at elements of the "nature of beauty." The sensation or the impression of beauty, he says, is universal and distinct from pleasure, relief, and gratification; even though these experiences have something in common, the "feeling of beauty" has a different quality: "Pure beauty drives those who are willing and able enough for its reception back into the depths of their inner self. It supersedes all their other interests, isolates them and makes them feel sad" (Sachs, 1940, p. 97).

He concludes that the sublimation of libido leads to an aesthetic experience of beauty, and he illustrates his idea with an enlightening story by Catulle Mendés:

one evening strolling through the streets of Paris he noticed a row of slot machines which for a small coin showed pictures of women in full or partial undress. He observed the leering interest with which men of all kind and description, well dressed and shabby, boys and old men, enjoyed the peep-show. He remarked that they all avoided one of these machines and wondering what uninteresting pictures it might show, he put his penny in the slot. To his great astonishment the generally shunned picture turned out to be the Venus of Medici. Now he begins to ponder: Why does nobody get excited about her? She is decidedly feminine and not less naked than the others which hold such strong fascination for everybody. Finally he finds a satisfactory answer: They fight shy of her because she is beautiful.

(Sachs, 1940, p. 95)

A certain inner process is required for the experience of beauty, according to Sachs. As the stimulation of sensual perception makes an id content acceptable to the ego, a feeling of peace and unity arises in the ego. And this, in turn, provides a narcissistic triumph not only for the ego but also for the superego – the triumph of having achieved the ideal of a complete, fully organized and functional personality. Through the superego, the representative of the death drive turned inward, the death drive plays an essential role in forming the aesthetic experience. Only because of the death drive, the aesthetic experience can endure and provide the beholder with the sublime feeling of peace inherent in it, explains Sachs.

When the influence of the stabilizing element provided by the death instinct is too weak or, expressing it the other way round, if the immediate demands of the Id have taken too prominent a part in the creation of the work or in the reactions of the beholder, reader or listener (mostly it will happen on both sides) then beauty is bound to give way either to an actual gratification or to the bitter feeling of frustration (e.g. a picture is too openly erotic and leads to either sex phantasies or a struggle against the stimulated desires). Nothing of that sort can happen when the death instinct – in this attenuated form – functions fully.

(1940, p. 132)

Ikonen and Rechardt (1978) seem to confirm Sachs' observation and elaborate it further when they say that experiences that have attained the correct form, perfection, timelessness, etc. are representations of Thanatos. The feeling that something is unbreakable, balanced, faultless, or

just right, that it should be preserved and not changed, means it is perceived as beautiful. In Sachs' words:

> The result is a feeling of restfulness and bliss, of having found, at least
> momentarily, a haven of peace where the external necessity to choose
> between sensual gratification and peace of mind is abolished. This is
> the reason why some little bit of beauty is such an indispensable help in
> carrying the burden of life.
>
> (1940, p. 133)

Hannah Segal comes to a slightly different conclusion because
of her different perspective regarding the death drive (1952, 1993).
She points to the importance of the other side of the death drive,
self-destruction and the destruction of objects, and maintains they
are as important for the experience of real beauty as is the notion
of life or the sexual drive. Only the contribution coming from death
drive tendencies provides the necessary terrifying experience of the
awesome aspects of a piece of art. The artist has to acknowledge the
death drive in both its aggressive and self-destructive aspects in
order to be able to symbolize it. And Segal stresses that for Sachs,
too, "every work of beauty still embodies the terrifying experience of
depression and death" (1952, p. 206). She points out that a satisfactory work of art is achieved through the realization and sublimation
of the depressive position, and that the "effect on the audience is that
they unconsciously re-live the artist's experience and share his triumph of achievement and his final detachment" (1952, p. 206). Only
when the depressive position has been worked through, one is able
to use symbols and to accept and to use one's death instinct and to
acknowledge death, Segal says. But she has a different idea regarding the role of the instincts in the aesthetic experience. "Re-stated in
terms of instincts, ugliness – destruction – is the expression of the
death instinct; beauty – the desire to unite into rhythms and wholes,
is that of the life instinct. The achievement of the artist is in giving the
fullest expression to the conflict and the union between those two"
(1952, p. 207). In the end, though, she cautiously arrives at the following idea: "It is tempting to suggest that this is so because in a great
work of art the degree of denial of the death instinct is less than in
any other human activity, that the death instinct is acknowledged, as
fully as can be borne. It is expressed and curbed to the needs of the
life instinct and creation" (1952, p. 207).

There are numerous examples of successful representations of destruction, death, dissolution, and aggression in film, theatre, dance, the visual arts, and music, where the form of the artwork "binds" the death drive and allows the creators to illustrate and perform with it phantasies connected with the death drive in order to bring them to consciousness, to reflect upon and to work through them as one of the primary functions of the arts in culture.

Hanns Sachs maintained that it is the static element in every work of art that provides the aesthetic experience. The form of a piece of art, the setting, the rhythm in music, drama, literature and poetry, and the formal aspects in the visual arts express this static element and thus represent a death drive quality. In terms of paintings, Wollheim distinguishes between formal and non-formal aspects of a painting, which together serve to create the representational content of a painting. And this can become – when the intention of the artist is fulfilled – the meaning of a painting for a sensitive spectator. Wollheim stresses that "the meaning of a painting is where we want it to be: neither in the head of the artist nor in the head of the spectator, but firmly on the surface of the painting" (1994, p. 36).

In this respect, the form of art, its static element, is important, as the achievement of poetry and every other piece of art lies not in the release of emotion but in its embodiment, according to Sachs. The formal aspect is indispensable for representing and embodying aggressive content as well as the more silent death drive aspects in cultural products. The form is a sublimated silent aspect of the death drive and secures the possibility to find expressions (i.e. thoughts, words, stories, and images) for the numerous "loud" aggressive aspects of it.

But also the negating, decathecting, unbinding, dissolving quality of the death drive, the "silent" death drive derivatives, which are hard to grasp because of the strong pull the unconscious has on them, have to be represented in every piece of art. Symbolizing the artist's working through, they are providing the beholder with the opportunity to do so, too. Examples of a more explicit embodiment of the quality of this part of the death drive could be seen in nihilism and existentialism in philosophy or in Goncharov's Oblomov, Melville's Bartleby, and Beckett's characters in literature, to name just a few.

On the one hand, the form of a work of art has a preserving and permanent quality that facilitates the representation of both life and death drive derivatives. On the other hand, though, the dissolution or negation of that form may be a sublimated expression of the silent part of the death drive, while the attacked or destroyed form may represent the louder part. This way, the form itself starts to carry meaning for the beholder. The pictorial language of abstract expressionism and several other formal expressions in the visual arts, the modernist avant-garde, the Nouveau Roman in literature, concrete poetry, or certain forms of drama and music seem to embody and represent the defusing, dissolving, or attacked structures.

In contrast to these successful sublimations and representations of death drive derivatives in the arts, an excessive defused death drive can undermine the capacity to represent, also in fields like thinking, ethics, and socialization. While life instincts lead to tension and involve a certain effort for the psychical apparatus, the death drives provide a pleasurable release and are therefore highly seductive. "The pleasure principle seems actually to serve the death instincts" (Freud, 1920, p. 63).

There are numerous attempts to define art and to differentiate pieces of art from "non-art" products. Taking into account the conditions mentioned previously about aesthetic experiences in the reception of art and the conditions of its production, one could attempt to approach these difficult questions from this point of view. Since aesthetic experiences are provided by the representation and sublimation of the fused sexual drive and death drive in various proportions, I would propose that the defusion of drives and an excess of the death drive, which aims to ease out any tension and seeks for undisturbed pleasure, brings about artificial products considered as "kitsch." They are produced in order to release any tension that is usually caused by the aesthetic experience of art or any other cultural achievement. In kitsch, an excess of unbound death drive leads to sentimentality instead of sentiment, hollowness instead of depth, complacency instead of beauty. As such, it is an expression of negation and not its representation as art would be.

Conclusion

The concept of the death drive was considered by Freud as theoretically indispensable for the dual concept of drives. It has its clinical relevance in masochism, negative therapeutic reaction, sense of guilt, and all the other mental states "beyond the pleasure principle," as Freud says: "These phenomena are unmistakable indications of the presence of a power in mental life which we call the instinct of aggression or of destruction according to its aims, and which we trace back to the original death instinct of living matter" (1937, p. 243).

The usual attribution of destructiveness to the death drive, up to the point of its equation to a "destructive instinct," as Freud sometimes did, makes it difficult to see and to take seriously its constructive, stabilizing, pacifying quality when it is limited by an adequate amount of libido in the individual but also in culture and civilization. Death drive derivatives are indispensable for many cultural achievements, and their tendency to negate and dissolve only becomes threatening for thoughts and structures when its perversion prevails and the fusion with life drives gets lost.

Therefore, I think, it is necessary to keep the concept of a death drive beyond the destructive drive and underscore its silent, releasing, stabilizing quality while at the same time also facing the regressive, negating, undermining, defusing, and defused activity of the "pure" death drive in both the individual and in culture.

Note

1   Throughout the chapter I will use the term "drive" as translation for Freud's "*Trieb*" for "sexual drive" and "death drive." The translation of "*Trieb*" into "instinct" will remain in citations. I will follow Strachey's translation "aggressive or destructive instinct" when Freud uses the term "*Destruktions- oder Aggressionstrieb*" in order to mark the conceptual differences between sexual drive/death drive and aggressive or destructive instinct.

References

Bell, D. L. (2015). The death drive: Phenomenological perspectives in contemporary Kleinian theory. *The International Journal of Psychoanalysis, 96*:411–423.

Britton, R., Chused, J., Ellman, S., & Likierman, M. (2006). Panel III: The role of attachment and love versus envy and destructiveness in the first year of life: Affects, impulses, and defenses. *Journal of Infant, Child, and Adolescent Psychotherapy, 5*:308–350.

Butler, J. (2014). On cruelty. *London Review of Books, 36*:31–33.

Folch, P., & de Folch, T. E. (1984). Report on the EPF-symposium on the death drive 1984. *EPF Bulletin, 22*:51–78.

Freud, S. (1905). *Three Essays on the Theory of Sexuality*. Standard Edition 7:123–246.

Freud, S. (1915). *Instincts and Their Vicissitudes*. Standard Edition 14:109–140.

Freud, S. (1920). *Beyond the Pleasure Principle*. Standard Edition 18:1–64.

Freud, S. (1923). *The Ego and the Id*. Standard Edition 19:1–66.

Freud, S. (1924). *The Economic Problem of Masochism*. Standard Edition 19:155–170.

Freud, S. (1930). *Civilization and Its Discontents*. Standard Edition 21:57–146.

Freud, S. (1937). *Analysis Terminable and Interminable*. Standard Edition 23:209–254.

Freud, S. (1940 [1938]). *An Outline of Psycho-Analysis*. Standard Edition 23:139–208.

Green, A. (1999). *The Work of the Negative*. London: Free Association.

Ikonen, P., & Rechardt, E. (1978). The vicissitudes of Thanatos: On the place of aggression and destructiveness in psychoanalytic interpretation. *Scandinavian Psychoanalytic Review*, 1:79–114.

Jones, E. (1957). *Sigmund Freud Life and Work (Volume Three: The Last Phase 1919–1939)*. London: The Hogarth Press.

Klein, M. (1932). *The Psycho-Analysis of Children*. London: The Hogarth Press.

Klein, M. (1946). Notes on some schizoid mechanisms. *The International Journal of Psychoanalysis*, 27:99–110.

Low, B. (1920). *Psycho-Analysis: A Brief Account of the Freudian Theory*. London: Allen & Unwin.

Sachs, H. (1940). Beauty, life and death. *American Imago*, 1:81–133.

Schmidt-Hellerau, C. (1995). *Life Drive & Death Drive, Libido & Lethe*. New York: Other Press.

Segal, H. (1952). A psycho-analytical approach to aesthetics. *The International Journal of Psychoanalysis*, 33:196–207.

Segal, H. (1993). On the clinical usefulness of the concept of death instinct. *The International Journal of Psychoanalysis*, 74:55–61.

Simmel, E. (1944). Self-preservation and the death instinct. *Psychoanalytic Quarterly*, 13:160–185.

Wollheim, R. (1994). *On Formalism and Its Kinds*. Barcelona: Fundació Antoni Tápies.

CHAPTER 7

In the name of Janus: do we need a dualistic drive theory?

August Ruhs

Death, life, and drive: Freudian speculations

Life and death are not only opposed to each other, they are inextricably knotted together. They form a unity in which life is determined by death and death defined by life. Living as a function of dying and dying as a function of living implies that the survival of an animalistic species marked by sexual reproduction concurs with the limitation of the existence of any of its individual members. Freud took up these considerations in his key essay "Beyond the Pleasure Principle," which, in turn, led to an extensive debate on the subject of human mortality in relation to sexual procreation (Freud, 1920). The entanglement of death and sexuality led Freud to enlarge and modify his drive theory by postulating a death drive alongside the sexual drive. The sexual and death drives were thought to be mostly in conflict with each other, nonetheless often acting in concert within the conception of a dualistic theory. The reasons for the introduction of a death drive were manifold. They included clinical facts, insights from anthropology and the cultural sciences, as well as metaphorical approximations. Freud was also influenced by the research of his colleagues, especially

Sabina Spielrein, August Stärcke, Otto Rank, Barbara Low, Wilhelm Stekel, Alfred Adler, and Theodor Reik (cf. De Vleminck, 2016).

The compulsion to repeat harmful and traumatic experiences ("*Wiederholungszwang*"), the negative therapeutic reaction, the guilt complex in neurosis, perverse ambitions and actions like sadism and masochism, the studies of schizophrenia and paranoia, and above all the dark face of death and nothingness in melancholia were insistent indications that not everything in life is regulated by the pleasure principle. Furthermore, Freud and his associates had from the beginning of psychoanalysis been aware of a range of other phenomena that spoke in favour of the entanglement of life and death, such as the conditions of animal sexuality, the phenomenon of entropy, as well as the notion of Nirvana within Buddhism as an expression of the ultimate liberation from both desire and suffering. Even the discovery of the unconscious existing alongside but also in the absence of consciousness was linked to a certain encounter with the death of the subject. Finally, many forms of acting out associated with the French expression of *passage-à-l'acte* show a subject's will to take upon the risk of death so as to maintain the feeling of being alive. This seemingly paradoxical phenomenon manifests itself in all religions that emphasize sacrifice as a necessary part of the exchange of life and death. This goes hand in hand with the conviction that real life is only possible in an afterworld, that is to say a life after death.

Given this background, it is legitimate to ask why it took two decades before an explicit and stringent conception of death as part of life penetrated psychoanalytic thinking and its theories. Perhaps it needed the horrifying experiences and consequences of World War I, as well as significant and tragic losses in his personal environment, for Freud to revise his metapsychological findings. This combined with an urge to modify his drive theory by postulating deadly and destructive drives as counterparts of libidinal and constructive drives.

Beyond doubt the interdependency of vitality and mortality was at the centre of Freud's thought right from the beginning. Still, many of Freud's successors were reluctant to take up his conception of a death drive as the last word in the development of psychoanalytic theory. This reticence can be understood, in part, as a resistance against the anxiety provoked by the threatening notion of "death." This resistance was at times powerful enough to contribute to the denial of the intelligibility of the effects and insistency of death (cf. Pommier, 2014, p. 11).

It is, however, not unlikely that the reticence was also related to Freud's occasional failure to sharply distinguish drives and instincts; a confusion often accentuated by some followers and especially by those who translated his texts into English. Freud was mostly very keen to differentiate the two notions, also in order to distinguish biological facts from psychological phenomena. He considered the latter the proper subject of psychoanalysis. But, notably, in the case of the death drive, he was less diligent in his differentiation, occasionally short-circuiting biological positions and the drive in its subjective internal dimensions of experienced urges, internal compulsions, and ardent desires. Freud himself criticized the inclination to subordinate the destructive forces to biological positions in his remarks to Sabina Spielrein's paper on the death instinct ("*Todesinstinkt*"). It was probably also for this reason that he cautiously labelled his new theories speculative. In other words, he was aware of the uncertain biological support for his clinical findings.

Civilization between lack of instincts, drive renunciation and sublimation

Freud's psychoanalytic theories of culture are centred on his insistence that culture is built upon prohibitions expecting from the individuals a renunciation of drives, a thesis he elaborated on in his essay "Civilization and Its Discontents" (Freud, 1930). From the clinical and individual perspective, this conclusion implies that those who are not able to modify their drive impulses are either criminals or perverse subjects – or else they take refuge in a neurosis with its unconscious compensations appearing as the negative of perversion. Freud's emphasis of renunciation as a key factor appears justified by the profound discomfort and discontents associated with the attainment of cultural achievements. That civilization should not primarily be based on gain but rather on frustration and lack, helps explain the unstable balance of societies and the permanence of cultural breakdowns as seen in collective hostilities and the acts of war.

Nevertheless, it is important to keep in mind that culture is not only based on a lack or a renunciation of satisfaction but also on the inherent deficiency of instincts, as these come to be substituted by human drives, in conjunction with the regulative forces of a civilization that is socially determined. This idea is based on the philosophies of anatomists and embryologists like Louis Bolk and Adolf Portman, who advanced the so-called fetalization theory, retardation theory, or neotenia. Such theories form part of "philosophical anthropology," a discipline founded in the 1920s. Based on the observation of human prematurity at birth, these theorists have argued that human development is less a consequence of a high level of evolution but more the result of an evolutional retardation. Besides Darwin's theory of evolution and creationism as its religious counterpart, this assertion represents a third point of view about the history of human origin.

Freud himself repeatedly referred to this topic, especially when he discussed the biological, phylogenetic, and psychological influences on the causation of neuroses:

> The biological factor is the long period of time during which the young of the human species is in a condition of helplessness and dependence. Its intra-uterine existence seems to be short in comparison with that of most animals, and it is sent into the world in a less finished state. As a result, the influence of the real external world upon it is intensified and an early differentiation between the ego and the id is promoted. Moreover, the dangers of the external world have a greater importance for it, so that the value of the object which can alone protect it against them and take the place of its former intra-uterine life is enormously enhanced. The biological factor, then, establishes the earliest situations of danger and creates the need to be loved which will accompany the child through the rest of its life.
>
> (Freud, 1926, pp. 154–155)

What is therefore specific about the human condition is not only that processes of civilization and cultural efforts result from and are always challenged by an abundance of drive forces that have to be repressed, tamed, and modified. The human situation is also specific by way of the inborn mechanisms hindering individuals to be autonomous immediately after birth, forcing them instead to rely on others for survival.

There are two opposing viewpoints about the origin of humans and human achievements within different psychoanalytic communities: one proposes that in the beginning there was the "word," as stated, for example, in the first book of Moses; the second considers it was the "deed," as argued by Goethe in his *Faust*. Here the "deed" refers to acts such as skills for using objects as tools, which eventually help their owners extricate themselves from the instinctual context. An impressive illustration of the second theorem is the opening scene of Stanley Kubrick's film *2001: A Space Odyssey* (1968), where an ape for the first time uses a bone to slay his kind. Freud, who characterized man a "prosthetic god," does not deny the importance of deeds in the history of humankind. However, he is more on the side of St. John and Moses, as shown in the following extract from 1893:

> Let us suppose that a man is insulted, is given a blow or something of the kind. This psychical trauma is linked with an increase in the sum of excitation of his nervous system. There then instinctively arises an inclination to diminish this increased excitation immediately. He hits back, and then feels easier; he may perhaps have reacted adequately – that is, he may have got rid of as much as had been introduced into him. Now this reaction may take various forms. For quite slight increases in excitation, alterations in his own body may perhaps be enough: weeping, abusing, raging, and so on. The more intense the trauma, the greater is the adequate reaction. The most adequate reaction, however, is always a deed. But, as an English writer has wittily remarked, the man who first flung a word of abuse at his enemy instead of a spear was the founder of civilization. Thus words are substitutes for deeds, and in some circumstances (e.g. in Confession) the only substitutes.
>
> (Freud, 1893, p. 36)

By defining culture as the institution of all efforts to reduce and limit the excess of drive forces, it follows that all drives have to undergo a process of transformation or domestication, since all drives are characterized by a tendency towards self-consummation, insofar as they aim at immediate satisfaction by way of rapidly dismounting tension thus concurrently fighting resistance against postponement and diversion. Still, Freud felt compelled to relativize this position, which is consistent with a monistic drive conception, thus renewing his inclination towards a dualistic drive theory marked by the dichotomy of sexual drives and death drives (Freud, 1920). He attached pleasure as well as vitality, constructive impulses, and the dimensions of love and desire to the libidinal drives, while allotting forms of experience that are beyond pleasure and which include destructive forces, aggression, violence, and hate to the death drives. He based this classification on two metaphysical assumptions: first, that living matter in the universe arises from lifeless material; and second, that every creature strives for returning to an inorganic state. The latter assumption is the quintessence of the so-called Nirvana principle. This dualism implies that when the death drive encounters the life drive, the latter assumes the task of disarming the effects of the destructive counterpart. This is, among other means, accomplished by the muscular system that is capable of deflecting the destructive forces onto the objects of the outer world (Freud, 1924). Thus, the death drive becomes the destructive aggressive drive, the drive of empowerment, the will to power (*"Wille zur Macht"*). Part of this destructive drive is put to the service of the sexual function and comes to represent sadism in its proper sense. Another part remains within the organism, is thus linked to libidinal energy, and comes to represent erotogenic masochism.

Freud concludes that the work of civilization and culture consists in taming and mitigating the rough and rude forces of the two drives, seen as a complex of an urge, stemming from a source in the organism and aiming at a specific satisfaction by means of particular objects. These efforts of transformation or domestication are, on the one hand, an operation upon the drive itself, something Freud called subli-mation, and, on the other hand, an operation concerning the object, qualified as idealization (cf. Freud, 1914, p. 94). In this regard, Freud observed that while in the ancient world the drives were glorified and cultivated, in our modern times the hallowing of objects is preponder-ant (Freud, 1905, p. 149). Whereas education, politics, and religion aim above all at taming, repressing, and reducing the forces emanating from drives, arts, literature, national customs, and other less repres-sive institutions allow partial drive satisfaction by way of sublimation and idealization.

When Freud was able to assimilate his final drive theory within his second topology, this brought the id to prominence. Keeping in mind a clear differentiation between drive and instinct, the id is that part of the personality that is the source of psychic energy in the form of the raw material of instinctual needs, prone to somatic influences, often a chaos, metaphorically succinctly described as "a cauldron full of seething excitations" (Freud, 1933, p. 73). Although this original energy is often considered both chaotic and destructive, it also provides the basis for taming cultural processes, which, in turn, implies that the repressions and sublimations of the deadening drives are managed by their own means. Therefore, the superego as the instance of internalized repres-sive forces always has at its core a basis of cruelty and violence, thereby contributing to the emergence of catastrophic aggression both in indi-viduals and in social groups. For instance, both religion and legislative institutions can function as taming instruments of aggression and sexuality, but they equally may cause atrocities such as religious wars, the death penalty, and so on. Furthermore, the decomposition of the drives may result in a predominance of the death drives as illustrated in melancholia, in which, following Freud, we experience the superego as the purest form of the death drive. Or shall we more generally say: the purest form of the drive in and of itself?

Perspectives on life and death by structural psychoanalysis

The two most important psychoanalytic currents after Freud, represented by Melanie Klein and Jacques Lacan, fully accepted the assumption of destructive drives as postulated by the ultimate Freudian drive theory, although both made differentiations and partly considerable modifications to the disputed conception of the death drive itself.

Melanie Klein assumes that already with its expulsive first cry, the primitive ego of the newborn has to stand up against the menacing forces of the death drive causing fear of invasive malevolence and anxiety of total annihilation. This is experienced as coming from the outside but ultimately derives from the outward projection of the death drive, thus causing a first splitting between an inner and an outer world. From this perspective, there is both an ego and an object from the onset of life, contrary to Freud's conception of an undifferentiated stage of primary narcissism. The possibility of integrating the two drives following splitting by way of re-integration of the destructive forces finally determines a good psychic balance and the well-being of the child. These processes not only mark two phases in the child's psychic development, known as paranoid-schizoid and depressive positions, they also represent states of mind that are present throughout life and can be reactivated at any time. Entangled with the drive's actions, primitive phantasies are understood as psychic realities and as unconscious expressions of the mental drives, albeit in accordance with an experience felt to be real. Not only the aggressive parts of the self but also the good and gratifying ones may be projected onto or into the object. This, in turn, is the basis for idealization. According to Klein, these projections of goodness and badness represent the operation of the life and the death drive, of love and hate (cf. Klein, 1932). Using this conceptual apparatus and above all by recognizing the widespread developmental failures of arriving at relatively stable depressive positions, many fatal and malign phenomena of contemporary societies can be explained.

Well disposed to Klein and her occupation with a concept of a real as an "unreal reality" (Klein, 1930, p. 221), Lacan also considers the death drive as a fundamental concept of psychoanalysis. He emphasizes that those who ignore the death drive in the psychoanalytic theory would have completely misunderstood its teaching (Lacan, 1960, p. 679). This affirmation, however, contains a fundamental alteration. According to Lacan, all biologically determined questions of life and death, such as being and passing away, or the urge of living substances to return to inanimate and inorganic states, do not belong to the category of drives. Lacan calls these *tendencies*. Especially in his seminar on ethics (Lacan, 1959–60), Lacan insists that the death drive is historically a concept of ethics that was/is central for shifting answers to the question of the *highest asset* (*summum bonum*) from Ancient Greece via Christianity to our modern times, revealing "a creationist thinking which opens up to an extraordinary rise of science, to modern atheism and to an unprecedented flourishing of the death drive in the heart of our civilisation" (Lauret, 2014, pp. 41–42, transl. A. Ruhs). One of the central figures of this development is de Sade, whose philosophy of cruelty, destruction, and death appears like an anticipated culmination of the theories of Nietzsche, Schopenhauer, Adorno, and, especially, Freud. Freud's conception of the "thing" – addressed four times in different essays (cf. Ruhs, 2017) – and his "science of desire," as psychoanalysis may be defined, serves Lacan as a basis for formulating a new *ultimate good*, an ultimate good that is detached from its cosmological bindings. From this perspective, the death drive is understood as "creationist sublimation" in the sense of pure desire transcending the consummation of drives in the framework defined by demand and enjoyment/*jouissance*.

These complex ideas are the result of Lacan's preoccupation with the death drive and human aggression from early on in his career as a psychoanalyst. His intention was to revoke the close association of drives to bio-physiological dimensions as hypothesized by Freud, when the latter used the metaphors of Eros and Thanatos. Between 1938 and 1950, Lacan elaborated on a theory linking the death drive to the order of the imaginary. After conceptualizing desire as the longing for a lost harmony and the craving to return to the pre-oedipal unity with the maternal breast and womb, he linked the death drive with the mirror stage of the infant's development and with the constitution of the ego by way of identifying with an image in the outer world, albeit with a highly alienating effect. This alienation is held to be the origin of aggressiveness corresponding to primary sadism and masochism.

In the context of the theory of the signifier as further elaborated in the 1950s, Lacan assigned the death drive to the symbolic order. Since the signifier is the "murder of the thing" (after Hegel's famous formulation) Lacan considers death as constitutive of the symbolic order, referring also to the assertion that the first symbol in the history of man is the tomb (Lacan, 1953). This leads him to conclude that we can have access to and a representation of death only by way of the signifier. By binding its existence to thinking and language, the subject can imagine the possibility of disappearing from the signifying chain by which it is constituted. But although the subject is regarded dead by way of the function of the signifier, it can reach immortality at the same time by way of the signifier. "Am I dead or alive?" is the unconscious question of the obsessional neurotic, who cannot stop thinking in order to preserve life. This idea echoes the famous one of Descartes, "cogito ergo sum." Descartes, too, saw the guarantee for being alive in thinking and reasoning.

Against this background, the death drive comes to represent the basic tendency of the symbolic order by way of repetition:

> And the death instinct is only the mask of the symbolic order, in so far – this is what Freud writes – as it is dumb, that is to say in so far as it hasn't been realised. . . . The symbolic order is simultaneously non-being and insisting to be, that is what Freud has in mind when he is talking about the death instinct as being what is most fundamental – a symbolic order in travail, in the process of coming, insisting on being realised.
>
> (Lacan, 1954–55, p. 326)

So it is by recognition and appropriation of the symbolic order, experienced as symbolic castration, that the subject can overcome the mortal silence of the drive and enter the paths of desire.

From the 1960s onwards and by elaborating the dimension of desire, Lacan began to distance himself from the Freudian dualistic theory. He did not consider desire as an inner movement but instead as originally experienced as coming from the outside – from the *object as cause of desire*. It constitutes the subject as a desired and a desiring one, a decentred subject looking for itself outside itself, searching for an object from which it has been separated and longing for finding this in order to find its own centre. Being at once a lack and a project, desire is situated between two poles: *desire of the Other* (whose discovery as a desiring Other may establish a relationship of love) on the one hand, and *desire of death* as the purest form of desire, on the other hand. According to Lacan, the latter's power and radicality is illustrated most notably in de Sade's *philosophy of the second death* and in the tragic figure of *Antigone* (Lacan, 1959–60).

Although Freud always insisted that what is primarily relevant for psychoanalysis is the psychological aspect of drive(s), that is to say the component that can be experienced by way of psychic representations, in his later writing he speculated about the biological foundations of the death drive, emphasizing the latter's relation to the Nirvana principle as a natural law applying to all organic creatures. By confronting and entangling the silent power of a primordial instinct-like drive with desire, and by proclaiming that the distinction between life and death drive, Lacan attempts to release the drive from its fixation on physical structures, so as to bring its historical dimensions to the foreground. Thereby, the original Freudian death drive is reformulated as a three-fold phenomenon in relation to the three fundamental categories of the real, the imaginary, and the symbolic: *tendency to death, willpower of death*, and *death drive*. The real dimension is related to the permanent repetitive striving for a return to the inanimate state (Nirvana principle), which Lacan calls a *tendency to death*. This is to be differentiated from the *willpower of death* (*volonté de la mort*), which designates annihilating forces steered by an acephalic drive submitted to a logic beyond both the pleasure principle and desire. The willpower of death strives for excess in the realm of enjoyment/*jouissance*, whereby pleasure is experienced as suffering. Finally, the *death drive* proper is a subjectized and reflected drive that is determined by the appropriation of the desire stemming from the *Other with capital O*. The functioning of this drive is co-extensive with the development of the symbolic order and the foundation of the unconscious, which might be regarded as a depository of repressed signifiers. However, the case of striving for death – of oneself or another – from the position of an object submitted to the desire of the Other, as experienced in cases of psychotic developments and especially in melancholia, does not fully capture the point. We can speak of the death drive in its entirety only insofar as the subject takes possession of the desire of the Other . . . thus no longer identifying it with a power imposed from outside. Because, above all, the subject must have separated from the Other, must have assumed by himself the risk of death, so that from then on the drive bears life and engagement in life.

(Pommier, 2014, p. 14, transl. A. Ruhs)

Approaches to this threshold have been referred to as *"disbeing"* (*desêtre*) and represent the end of an analysis. In such cases, the subject is confronted with the inhuman regions of the "thing" as a kind of proto-representation. After having passed the questions raised by the destinies of Oedipus and Antigone as well as all the phantasies containing the imaginary identifications with the partial objects, the subject can find his being for himself, which will be a liberated self.

Leaving behind enjoyment/*jouissance*, which represents the satisfaction of a drive beyond pleasure, and having undergone symbolic castration, the death drive as desire of death can be thought of as a process of sublimation, following Lacan's definition of sublimation as the elevation of the object to the dignity of the "thing." The "thing" as a sovereign asset and ultimate aim of desire is the central void around which the chain of the signifiers is organized, representing a point of particular attraction in ethics and in aesthetics, in arts as well as in the domains of beauty, courtly love, and other higher efforts of creativity striving for access to that what lies behind obvious appearances and perceptions. This also includes the twisted striving for an ultimate evil as is proved by the history of mankind and developments in some individuals.

Regarding the intellectual world of de Sade, which provides elucidations for manifold perverse acts of mortal cruelty as well as templates of individual and collective manifestations of severe pathologies of the self, Lacan stresses the concept of the death drive as a "creationist sublimation" aiming at a twofold death and an absolute destruction. Based on the principle that human beings should collaborate with the creations of nature – a concept also present in the ethics of Spinoza – de Sade emphasizes the human participation in the destructive and dissolving tendencies that are necessary for nature to fulfil the task of new creations. It is by the worst crimes and the most abominable atrocities and cruelties that these ambitions can be reached, aiming at a total annihilation as expressed in de Sade's novel *Juliette, or Vice Amply Rewarded*:

> For doing an even better service [to nature] it would be necessary to oppose the regeneration of the corpse which we are burying. The murder just takes away the first life of the individual we are hitting; one should be able to snatch his second one in order to be even more useful to nature; because it is annihilation that it wants.
>
> (cited after Lauret, 2014, p. 65, transl. A. Ruhs)

It seems that in our funeral ceremonials, procedures like cremation as a final destruction in the sense of a second death instead of burying the cadavers are an expression of these phantasies, representing aspirations for an absolute death or at least of our bodily existence.

On the other hand, Antigone appears as the central character in Sophocles' tragedy, which, like all tragedies on stage, aims to tame and pacify passion through catharsis. Intimately entangled with her tyrannical and criminal brother, Antigone embodies a desire of death, whose criminal gloom finds its counterpart in her dazzling beauty. Without discussing all the details of this tragedy full of crimes, incestuous liaisons, and severe guilt that have befallen the Labdacides family, Antigone, the daughter of Oedipus and Jocasta, takes upon herself the risk of death when she refuses to submit to the interdiction to bury the corpse of her brother, who was inculpated of high treason and fratricide. Antigone dies a second time after suffering a psychic death through the crimes of her family. It is by her beauty, whose glance is vividly expressed by the chorus as a theatrical means of emotionality, that this central image charged with desire can fade out all the other images of cruelty and murder forcing Antigone to desire her death.

Another aspect of the death drive appearing as a desire of death is presented by Lacan in his speech at the Catholic University of Louvain (Belgium) in 1972. Here he asserts that death is a matter of belief and hope that is shared by the unconscious, which thus affirms the certainty of death that is repressed by the subject. He claims that the prospect of an eternal life is in itself unbearable and would, if it were to materialize, lead to psychosis:

> Death belongs to the domain of belief. You are completely right to believe that you shall certainly die; it keeps you going. If you did not believe, could you bear the life you lead? If one could not rest on this certainty, that there will be an end, could you bear the whole matter? Nevertheless, it is only a matter of the act of believing; but the worst of the worst is that you are not sure at all. Why should it not be possible that some one

or another lives 150 years, but anyway, in the end it is the belief which is powerful here . . . one of my patients . . . dreamt one day that existence would again and again pour out of itself, the dream of Pascal so to speak, an infinity of life, always succeeding itself without a possible end; she was nearly mad when she woke up, as she was telling me.

(Lacan, 1972, transl. A. Ruhs)

From this perspective, Freud's early views on death, destruction, and war (Freud, 1915), where he claims that we wish the death of foreigners and enemies, whilst blinding ourselves to the fact of our own death by phantasies of immortality, cannot be the last word. Instead, the death drive as elaborated in "Beyond the Pleasure Principle" (1920) implies not only a biological fact but also a silent longing for dying. As Freud always used to point out, we cannot grasp the essence of the drive but have access to it only as a phenomenon, via psychic representations belonging to the realm of the imaginary and the order of the symbolic. Via passing through the constriction of the signifying chain (i.e. symbolic castration), the primordial and rude drive forces in the sense of partial drives in their relation to the primordial objects, which belong to the unconscious of the real and are marked by enjoyment/*jouissance* and repetition, are transformed into pleasure and desire. In their co-extension, language and desire are monistic areas. As already mentioned, enjoyment/*jouissance* as well as pleasure are beyond the ethics of good and evil, beyond constructive and destructive conscious thoughts and acts. Therefore, a dualistic drive theory is dispensable. Supported by the belief of the mortality of our bodies and minds, we can more easily dream of another immortality, namely that of our traces on earth, as it survives in legends, grounded in the legacy of an oeuvre or in the inscriptions of a tombstone.

References

De Vleminck, J. (2016). Der Todestrieb, ein psychoanalytischer Fremdkörper? Metapsychologie und Klinik. *texte. psychoanalyse. ästhetik. kulturkritik*, 36:465–490.

Freud, S. (1893). *On the Psychical Mechanism of Hysterical Phenomena*. Standard Edition 3:25–39.

Freud, S. (1905). *Three Essays on the Theory of Sexuality*. Standard Edition 7:123–246.

Freud, S. (1914). *On Narcissism: An Introduction*. Standard Edition 14:67–102.

Freud, S. (1915). *Thoughts for the Times on War and Death*. Standard Edition 14:273–300.

Freud, S. (1920). *Beyond the Pleasure Principle*. Standard Edition 18:1–64.

Freud, S. (1924). *The Economic Problem of Masochism*. Standard Edition 19:155–170.

Freud, S. (1926). *Inhibitions, Symptoms and Anxiety*. Standard Edition 20:75–176.

Freud, S. (1930). *Civilization and Its Discontents*. Standard Edition 21:57–146.

Freud, S. (1933). *New Introductory Lectures on Psycho-Analysis*. Standard Edition 22:1–182.

Klein, M. (1930). The importance of symbol-formation in ego development. In: *Love, Guilt and Reparation and Other Works 1921–1945* (pp. 219–232). London: The Hogarth Press and the Institute of Psycho-Analysis, 1975.

Klein, M. (1932). *The Psycho-Analysis of Children*. London: The Hogarth Press, 1975.

Lacan, J. (1953). The function and field of speech and language in psycho-analysis. In: *Ecrits: The First Complete Edition in English* (pp. 197–268). New York: WW Norton, 2006.

Lacan, J. (1954–55). *The Ego in Freud's Theory and in the Technique of Psycho-analysis (The Seminar of Jacques Lacan, Book II)*. New York: WW Norton, 1988.

Lacan, J. (1959–60). *The Ethics of Psychoanalysis (The Seminar of Jacques Lacan, Book VII)*. New York: WW Norton, 1986.

Lacan, J. (1960). The subversion of the subject and the dialectic of desire in the Freudian unconscious. In: *Ecrits: The First Complete Edition in English* (pp. 671–702). New York: WW Norton, 2006.

Lacan, J. (1972). Conférence à Louvain, le 13 octobre 1972. In: www.valas.fr/Jacques-Lacan-Conference-a-Louvain-le-13-octobre-1972,013; called up on November 6, 2017.

Lauret, M. (2014). *L'énigme de la pulsion de mort. Pour une éthique de la joie*. Paris: Presses Universitaires de France.

Pommier, G. (2014). Foreword. In: M. Lauret (Ed.), *L'énigme de la pulsion de mort. Pour une éthique de la joie*. Paris: Presses Universitaires de France.

Ruhs, A. (2017). Zum Ding bei Freud und Lacan als Urerfahrung von Fremdheit. In: U. Kadi, S. Schlüter & E. Skale (Eds.), *Fremd. Im eigenen Haus. Sigmund-Freud-Vorlesungen 2016* (pp. 23–34). Vienna: Mandelbaum.

PART IV
HISTORY

CHAPTER 8

The drive that silences: the death drive and the oral transmission in Viennese psychoanalysis

Daru Huppert

On March 13, 1938, on the same day of the official annexation of Austria by Nazi Germany, a meeting took place at the Viennese Psychoanalytical Society. Those attending the meeting agreed that all members of the society who were able to do so should flee from Austria and follow Freud, to wherever he would settle. Faced with the possible destruction of Viennese psychoanalysis, Freud invoked a stirring comparison:

> After the destruction of the Temple in Jerusalem by Titus, Rabbi Jochanan ben Sakkai asked for permission to build the first Torah school in Jabneh for the study of the Thora. We are going to do the same. We are, after all, used to persecution by our history, tradition and some of us through our personal experiences.
>
> (Jones, 1957, p. 236)

This was a deeply resonant comparison. Rabbi ben Sakkai was the founder of Talmudic Judaism, a tradition that is based on the interpretation of the Torah (the Five Books of Moses) and its commentaries. It is because of this tradition that Judaism is believed to have survived in exile and to have become the Religion of the Book, with the Old Testament serving as the "portable fatherland" (Heine, 1979, p. 43, my translation) of the Jews. Thus, when Freud referred to Rabbi ben Sakkai, he was evoking the central figure of Judaism's survival under conditions of defeat, exile, suppression, and persecution. In view of the Nazis' murderous antisemitism, this reference was as poignant as it was defiant.

It is startling that in a situation of so drastic a threat to psychoanalysis, Freud should draw on a tradition that survived by investing itself in the interpretation of its fundamental texts. This was more than a flight into magical thinking. Freud was not simply invoking a past so distant that it had become mythological. Nor was he, faced with the Nazi terror, lapsing into an idolatry of his tribe. If we are to understand the implications of Freud's reference to Rabbi ben Sakkai, we need to bear in mind the principles of Talmudic interpretation. In this practice, the fundamental texts are elucidated in a group setting through a discussion that is often fervent and contested. It is contested because the meanings of the texts are not assumed to be given, but in need of discovery by those engaged in the discussion. The interpreters are called on to use all their imaginative capacities to discover those meanings of the texts that enable them to make sense of their actual situation. Through this engagement the group is led to produce determinate, highly invested interpretations, whilst understanding that these interpretations in no way exhaust the potential meanings of the texts themselves. An assumption of this practice is that the vitality of a group depends on its ability to draw on and develop the insights of the fundamental teachings it possesses. Indeed, this practice is seen as the principal factor in shaping the group; indeed, interpretation of this kind is assumed to be what preserves and develops a form of life. Freud was aware of these features of Talmudic practice (cf. Hegenauer, 2017). So when he referred to the founding of a new school of Torah, he was implying that a similar interpretative engagement would allow the Viennese psychoanalytic lineage – and, perhaps, psychoanalysis as a whole – to survive in conditions that threatened its existence. This kind of practice, as I would interpret Freud's hopes, might prevent the external terror from unleashing an internal process of dissolution within the Viennese psychoanalytic lineage.

Since we are concerned with the possible survival or demise of a psychoanalytic lineage, it seems apposite to draw on Freud's theory of the drives. This theory is his most basic frame of reference for addressing the psychological forces involved in the life and death not only of human beings but also of their enterprises. Recourse to the drive theory makes it evident that the interpretative engagement Freud was envisioning along Talmudic lines would be a work of Eros, whose principle task is to avert the disintegrating operation of the death drive. Talmudic interpretation of Freud's writings (though, of course, not only these) would serve to unite the Viennese Group – and perhaps psychoanalysts more generally.[1] At a deeper level of analysis, the task of such interpretative engagement would be to bind – that is, countervail – the death drive operating within the psychoanalytic transmission itself. My assumption is that the death drive – its silently eviscerating work – is always operating in the transmission of psychoanalysis and requires a constant effort – the work of Eros – to be overcome. This, of course, is not unique to our discipline. Rather, it is general feature of any discipline that depends primarily on a verbal transmission. However, under circumstances that are not excessively disruptive, we can usually disregard the eviscerating effects of this drive on the transmission of a lineage, as these effects are mostly countervailed by the work of Eros. In such cases, the lineage is passed on, evolves, and changes; it is not silenced. But the situation described at the outset of the essay was disruptive, indeed traumatically so. The Nazi terror threatened to unleash a process of disintegration within, at least, the Viennese lineage of psychoanalysis. In fact, the forced dispersal of the early Viennese psychoanalysts eventually led to a near total neglect of their work. I take this *neglect* to be a drastic, though largely unnoticed, effect of the death drive released in our discipline by the traumatic nature of the Nazi attack. That is the first issue I want to discuss. In this chapter, I also want to examine a more general, less severe, though nevertheless insidious effect of this drive in what I will describe as our *malaise* in relation to Freud's work. I take this malaise to be influenced, in part, by the neglect of the early Viennese tradition. Because the issues I will discuss here are exceedingly complex, I will provide only a minimal account. It is only the starkness of my account that will allow me to present my ideas with some measure of clarity.

The lineage of Viennese psychoanalysis and its neglect

In the meeting of the Viennese Psychoanalytical Society on March 18, 1938, as we have seen, Freud expressed his hope that the members of the Society would settle where he would. This may seem strange and in need of interpretation. In "Moses and Monotheism," Freud, already in London and approaching his death in the next year, would declare that "psychoanalysis, which in the course of my long life has gone everywhere, still possesses no home that could be more valuable for it than the city in which it was born and grew up" (1939, p. 55). In this statement, Freud was not singing his own praise. He was expressing – as he rarely did – his appreciation for the work of his Viennese colleagues. These colleagues included figures such as Paul Federn, Otto Fenichel, Helene Deutsch, Wilhelm Reich, Franz Alexander, August Aichhorn, and, of course, his daughter Anna. The body of work produced by this group is as engaging and insightful as any in the rich history of psychoanalysis. Yet, Freud's wish that this group should stay together is, I believe, conditioned by a more specific feature of their writings: their work was, to a unique degree, an extension and development of his ideas. They developed *the form of thought* that Freud had initiated. It is this feature that gives a family resemblance to the otherwise diverse writings of the Viennese Group. The members of this group had, in particular, developed great skill in extending his clinical ideas to fields that he had not studied in depth, such as psychosis, what today we call borderline conditions, femininity, and wayward youths. They had also developed a unique sense of the clinical urgency of Freud's metapsychological ideas.

It is therefore hardly surprising that reading their work often provides us with a clearer notion of certain themes in Freud's work than his own texts. The intimacy of the Viennese Group with Freud's writings arose not only from reading his texts but also, to make my Talmudic point, from a continual discussion of them. Much of their work arose from a direct or indirect debate with him. We might say that Freud was their discussion. I do not, however, want here to engage in a sentimental idealization of the Viennese Group. There were many and well-known tensions in this group, leading, in some cases, to defections. Moreover, the members of this group tended to treat the work of other psychoanalytic lineages with a sense of arrogant dismay (for examples of this, see Aichhorn in this book). What I hope to convey is simply that when Freud thought of establishing a new Torah school, his hope was to recreate the Viennese situation. He trusted the Viennese Group sufficiently to develop psychoanalysis in a way that reflected the fundamental intentions embodied in his writings. As the Talmudic model suggests, this required them staying together as a group. One might object that I am making too strong a claim for the homogeneity of the early Viennese lineage. But I am not claiming that the members of the Viennese Society formed a uniform group; my idea is simply that their work showed the same kinds of resemblance that allows us to speak of the "Kleinian" school in London, or the school of "Ego Psychology" in New York. What I do wish to emphasize is that the lineages of psychoanalysis are highly dependent on the congregation of a particular group, in a particular location – in this sense, psychoanalysis is very much a local affair. That is why, I suggest, Freud wanted his group to stay together in one place.

Freud hoped in vain. The early Viennese lineage of psychoanalysis came to a sudden end, or rather, it was terminated by the Nazis. Some of its members were murdered and most others forced to migrate wherever they could. Several of them – such as Anna Freud and Heinz Hartmann, to name but two – came to exert a profound influence on other psychoanalytic cultures. But this is not to be confused with the development of the Viennese lineage. The Viennese lineage itself terminated suddenly and traumatically with the dispersal of its members. How serious a loss this was, and continues to be, is rarely emphasized. Within the psychoanalytic community in Vienna today, the work of this group forms only a negligible part of our discussion or of our psychoanalytic training. It is disturbing that the psychoanalysts who were forced to leave Vienna by the Nazis are today mostly ignored by those of us who currently practise psychoanalysis in this city and who stand in their line of succession. This situation requires interpretation. Recourse to the death drive can elucidate some of its more insidious features. Before I attempt to show this, I will present a highly condensed and abstracted account, or rather a construction, of how this neglect came about. It might seem that history, rather than construction, is what we need. But a more complete historical account might occlude the point I want to make.[2]

After the war, the few psychoanalysts of the Viennese Group who had remained in the city, and the even fewer who returned, could not make up for the loss of those who had gone, nor could they, by themselves, represent this formidable tradition. Their attachment to this lineage, whose loss was deeply personal to them, may have hampered their ability to pass on its urgent quality and the need to develop such works further. Thus, inadvertently, they may have contributed to a fossilization of the work they had sought to pass on. Death by entombment is a danger to which traditions are always vulnerable, particularly after they have been almost mortally weakened. On the other side, the new generations of psychoanalysts were faced with a formidable body of work by the original Viennese Group, a body of work that is demanding and not easy to assimilate. Moreover, this was a past too great for the newer generations to hope to extend by themselves. To make matters worse, those members of the Viennese Group who no longer lived in Vienna loathed to return to the city from which they had been banished (cf. Aichhorn in this book). Thus, the early Viennese analysts did not convey the intimate meanings of their writings through oral transmission. As time progressed, other powerful conceptions of psychoanalysis became increasingly available. These conceptions developed from intact lineages and seemed to offer more directly relevant clinical or theoretical orientation, not least because those propounding these lineages could transmit them orally through discussions, lectures, supervisions, and the like. Over time the theoretical allegiances in Vienna moved towards these other lineages and this, in turn, made it more difficult to understand the writings and concerns of the Viennese Group. In such an account, there is nothing strange about the Viennese Group falling to the wayside. Lineages, like families, disappear.

However, it seems to me that something more disturbing is at work in the neglect of the early Viennese lineage. As suggested earlier, certain aspects of this neglect can be elucidated if we take seriously the idea that the death drive is at work in the very process of psychoanalytic transmission. I can approach this idea only indirectly.

The death drive and non-transmission

In "Civilization and Its Discontents," Freud (1930) explores the possibility that no experience of the individual psyche is forgotten or disappears completely. He concludes that the preservation of what is psychical is the norm, but he seems to allow for exceptions in the case of traumatic experiences (ibid., p. 71). Although Freud does not pursue this line of inquiry very far, he suggests that certain traumatic experiences really do get lost and are not merely repressed. This may lead to gaps or holes in the psyche. An analogous process, I suggest, may operate in groups, particularly in the transmission of a lineage from one generation to the next.[3] Accounts of intergenerational transmission of traumatic experiences have mostly focused on how descendants of individuals who have suffered severe traumatization unconsciously identify with and compulsively repeat certain features of the disruptive experience suffered by the earlier generation (Faimberg, 1988; Laub & Lee, 2003). To give a glaring example: a man whose family members were killed in an extermination camp tries to commit suicide by using a gas stove, without consciously realizing the link between his act and the annihilation of his family (Huppert, 2007). Such occurrences have given rise to the claim that trauma has been *transposed* from one generation to the next. Here I want to emphasize a related but inverse phenomenon, which might be called *negative* repetition: what is repeated in this case is not a particular feature of the traumatic event but the attempt to evade this event as thoroughly as possible. Such attempts can succeed if two conditions are satisfied: (1) the person or the group ceases to understand themselves as part of a lineage that has suffered a traumatic experience and (2) they are unconscious of having severed this link. When these conditions are met, even if only partly, this produces gaping holes in the intergenerational transmission. The neglect of the Viennese Group is a case in point, and recourse to the death drive seems necessary to help comprehend the non-transmission of their work.

This should come as no surprise, for there are intimate links between the death drive and traumatic situations in the individual (Baranger, Baranger, & Mom, 1988). Summarily put, the traumatic situation alters the relationship between the drives, leading to an unbinding and therefore to an unleashing of the death drive. In groups, an analogous effect may take place when the group is attacked and dissolved. The forces that would allow for the survival of the group or of a lineage are diminished, while those forces working towards its extinction are strengthened. So let us now turn to the specific operation of the death drive. A principle effect of this drive is that once released it further unbinds libidinal relationships (Freud, 1920), that is, it leads to a drastic form of libidinal disinvestment (Green, 1999). Experientially, this manifests as a withdrawal of affect culminating in indifference. But by its very nature such a development may go unnoticed. Freud emphasized that the death drive operates unobtrusively (1920, p. 63) and mutely (1923, p. 47), so that its effects may escape perception. When we translate the process of unbinding to groups, we find that this unbinding produces an interruption or a gap in the line of transmission. The death drive severs the link between generations, and this contrasts with what we might call an oedipal genealogy. In the latter, the descendants try to vanquish the preceding generation but subsequently identify with fundamental features of the generation they attempt to overcome. In the genealogy I am trying to outline, the earlier generation is disinvested by the later one. As a result, the preceding generation is neglected and becomes irrelevant; they cease to be our past. What takes place is a non-transmission.

As I see it, the neglect of the early lineage of Viennese psychoanalysis is partly determined by the very process of unbinding just described. So when, after the war, later generations of psychoanalysts evinced an apparently usual disinterest in the work of the Viennese Group, I contend that this disinterest was overdetermined by a more insidious form of indifference. Similarly, what was felt by these generations to be a more or less considered choice, that of disengaging with the writings of the Viennese Group, was also an erasure of this body of work through disinvestment. Entering a lineage requires a certain degree of identification with it. But it is uncanny to enter into a lineage was eradicated, particularly when this traumatic event occurred in the near past. What instead took place in Vienna is a form of disidentification with the Viennese Group; one might here speak of a disidentification with the persecuted. Over time the cumulative effect of many small disengagements and disidentifications led to the nigh total neglect of the Viennese Group. As a result of this, we are today in Vienna, formally speaking, the successors to the early Viennese Group, from which in fact we are almost entirely estranged. That this glaring situation is hardly perceived and not felt to be disturbing is itself an effect of the death drive. This drive operates like an anaesthetic: not only does it numb us, it also makes us unaware that we no longer feel anything.

Given the general neglect of the early Viennese lineage, the efforts of the historical work group (discussed in the following chapters), which researches the individual lives and the writings of the early Viennese psychoanalysts, are of utmost importance. These efforts may help redress some of the indifference I have tried to depict. While the direct lineage of the Viennese Group has disappeared and cannot be revived, their writings remain and demand our study. It is difficult to write about what can be gained by immersing ourselves in abandoned lines of development without sounding overly sententious. Some of the gains are deflationary. Reading the writings of the Viennese Group can weaken our tendency to overestimate the necessity of our own theoretical preferences. Our appreciation of the outstanding quality of the early work tends to moderate the exaggerated views we hold of our own achievements; it diminishes, to use an ugly phrase for an unsavoury phenomenon, the narcissism of the now. On a bleaker note, engaging with these writings can alert us to the stark reality that ours is a precarious discipline. We come to see that the development of psychoanalysis is deeply affected by contingent factors, such as the ravages of history and also, though more discretely, the operations of the death drive within this discipline itself.

Yet, probably these deflationary effects are part of the reason why we so rarely read the work of the Viennese Group in the first place. So I hasten to emphasize that engaging with their work is also deeply stimulating. Psychoanalysis, as a therapy of the individual, is committed to providing access to abandoned and thwarted lines of development. Just as in the case of the individual, the abandoned lines of our discipline often contain issues of great urgency and importance that are in need of development. Studying the early Viennese discourse is therefore not an exercise in antiquarianism. There are many buried treasures in the early Viennese writings, whose excavation has the potential to enrich psychoanalysis here and now.[4] But the gain is also of a more general kind. Recourse to the work of the Viennese Group, which posed questions and raised issues we no longer address, can provide us with an expanded sense of possibility about what psychoanalysis is. While the early Viennese lineage has disappeared, its writings can still become part of our debate.

Our malaise with Freud

I now would like to claim that the neglect of the Viennese Group has conditioned our relationship to Freud's writing. A similar, though by no means as drastic a disinvestment is also prevalent amongst practising psychoanalysts with regards to his writings. It manifests in a sense of malaise about Freud's work, particularly about its clinical relevance. This malaise is atmospheric rather than being explicit; nevertheless, it is real and pernicious. One factor influencing this malaise is that we often lack models of how to extend his clinical work. Such models could be found in the writings of the Viennese Group, but these we neglect. The sense of disorientation we experience in regard to Freud is not confined to Vienna, but is much more widespread. And although there exist many examples to the contrary, this malaise is prevalent enough for it to require interpretation.

My claim might seem absurd. Few disciplines, if any, seem to be more obsessed with its founder than psychoanalysis. The majority of psychoanalytic articles in international journals begin with some reference to Freud, but more often than not Freud is referred to, only then to be ignored. Moreover, I am here primarily concerned with the manner in which Freud's writings are taught and discussed in psychoanalytic institutions. It is through such oral transmission that we develop our sense of what psychoanalysis is and of what, as psychoanalysts, we are supposedly doing. It is here that I see a disjunction. On the one hand, Freud's writings are presented as the foundation of our discipline and as its greatest achievement. On the other, they are treated as if they possessed only remote clinical significance. His work on particular phenomena, such as dreams, is seen to be too intricate, his metapsychology is deemed too abstract, and his cultural writings are held to be largely irrelevant for the clinic. As for his clinical writings, they are considered distant and no longer applicable to most patients we treat. No one would put this so drastically, but often much of the preceding, even all of it, is implied. In this way Freud's writings have acquired the confusing status of being both fundamental and irrelevant, vital and inconsequential. To vary an aphorism of Freud's (1921, p. 91) concerning mankind's relationship to great thinkers: while we pretend to admire Freud, we do not take him seriously.

This situation reflects an ambivalence in our relation to Freud. Our veneration for his work is coupled with a covert but deep tendency to denigrate it. Psychoanalysis has powerful resources to understand this state of affairs. We might, for example, infer that this ambivalence is the product of parricidal rage against Freud, combined with the necessity to conceal this passion through signs of veneration. I would like to emphasize that no one is free from this kind of ambivalence. Such are the passions that all flesh is heir to. But next to the violent motivations such as these that condition our malaise, there are other motivations that are more banal and, perhaps, more insidious. Is not the covert denigration of Freud's theory an invitation to disengage with it? Such an invitation would be the manifest side of a tendency to libidinally disinvest his work, ultimately leading to indifference, which is a derivative expression of the death drive. There are, of course, many reasons for this disinvestment, but the unnoticed demise of the Viennese Group is certainly an important factor, for it was the lineage that was most intimate with his writings and with the demands they place on us. Once again, a central issue in our malaise with Freud is that the death drive, and its derivative expressions, operates discretely. Our libidinal and thus emotional investments are withdrawn without our awareness of this dissolution having occurred. This helps to explain why our malaise in relationship to Freud may go unnoticed, or seem inconsequential. Its expressions are banal. Cumulatively, however, these expressions can render hollow our relationship to the very work that contains the fundamental insights of psychoanalysis. The effects of the death drive are contrary to those of the phantom limb; the latter hurts us, even though it is no longer present, whereas the death drive makes us not feel what we urgently lack.

Reinvestment

My argument has been that the neglect suffered by the Viennese Group and our malaise with Freud are, in part, an effect of the silent work of the death drive. If this is correct, if only approximately, it needs redressing. What form that might take is difficult to outline. The Talmudic approach offers two useful suggestions. The first is that the vitality of a tradition is to a large degree dependent on an engagement, that is, a libidinal investment of its foundational texts. The second is that the onus is on us to make sense of our experience through these texts. Freud's writings, in particular, require Talmudic interpretation. They demand an ongoing communal discussion, and, in a wider sense, they *are* this discussion, for they cannot be understood without the often extraordinary efforts undertaken to develop them. The texts of the Viennese Group are one principal effort of this kind.

On a more general level, I have tried to show that the forces studied by psychoanalysis – ultimately the drives – operate in the discipline itself and particularly in the process of its verbal transmission. This is not just true for the libidinal drive but also for its disintegrating counterpart. We are accustomed to recognize the death drive in its more extreme effects. But some of its effects are banal and this might help to explain why Freud took so long to discover this drive. Neglect is not a dramatic reaction, nor is indifference. Their effects, however, can be dismal, as seen in the abandonment of the early Viennese lineage. In view of such results, the Talmudic proposal of an ongoing discussion of our basic texts becomes compelling. Such communal discussion can be difficult and even exasperating. But it can also be exuberant. That is why I want to end by quoting a letter that Freud (2008) wrote to Grodeck, which inimitably conveys this sense of exhilaration.

> It is difficult to practice psychoanalysis alone. It is an exquisitely gregarious enterprise. It would be much more beautiful if we could roar and howl with each other in chorus and in the same rhythm, rather than everyone grumbling alone for himself.
>
>   (p. 216, translated for this edition)

Perhaps such moments of exhilaration are our best bet against the discreet lures of indifference that are always at work in our discipline.

Notes

1   I am aware that this interpretation may appear to be deeply conservative, clashing with the more empirical notion that psychoanalysis develops out of the requirements of our clinical experience. But I would argue that these tasks are less separate than they might appear and that, at the very least, they are complementary. Both are required.
2   For a historical account of the Viennese Psychoanalytical Society during and after the war, see Wiener Psychoanalytische Vereinigung (2005).
3   This move from the individual to the group may appear to be a leap but, as Freud (1921, p. 69) emphasized in his group psychology, the psychological demarcations between the individual and the group are not very sharp. Frequently, individual and group psychology offer what are merely two perspectives on the same phenomenon.
4   In my own research, resort to the early Viennese tradition has allowed me to take up abandoned themes in psychoanalysis, such as sleep (Huppert, 2018a) and disgust (Huppert, 2018b), both of which are of considerable clinical significance.

References

Baranger, M., Baranger, W., & Mom, J. (1988). The infantile psychic trauma from us to Freud. *International Journal of Psychoanalysis, 69*:113–128.

Faimberg, H. (1988). The telescoping of generations. *Contemporary Psycho-analysis, 24*:99–117.

Freud, S. (1920). *Beyond the Pleasure Principle*. Standard Edition 18:1–64.

Freud, S. (1921). *Group Psychology and the Analysis of the Ego*. Standard Edition 18:65–144.

Freud, S. (1923). *The Ego and the Id*. Standard Edition 19:1–66.

Freud, S. (1930). *Civilization and Its Discontents*. Standard Edition 21:57–146.

Freud, S. (1939). *Moses and Monotheism*. Standard Edition 24:1–138.

Freud, S. (2008). *Briefwechsel. Georg Grodeck – Sigmund Freud*. Frankfurt am Main: Stroemfeld.

Green, A. (1999). *The Work of the Negative*. London: Free Association Books.

Heine, H. (1979). Zur Geschichte der Religion und Philosophie in Deutschland. In: *Historisch Kritische Gesamtausgabe der Werke*. Hamburg: Hoffmann und Campe.

Hegenauer, W. (2017). *Heilige Texte*. Gießen: Psychosozial Verlag.

Huppert, D. (2007). *The Destruction of Psychic Reality*. Unpublished dissertation.

Huppert, D. (2018a). Am Schlaf der Welt rühren. *Zeitschrift für psychoanalytische Theorie und Praxis*, in press.

Huppert, D. (2018b). Der Pelz der Venus im Kot. In: *Sigmund Freud Vorlesungen 2017* (pp. 207–217). Vienna: Mandelbaum Verlag.

Jones, E. (1957). *Sigmund Freud Life and Work (Volume Three: The Last Phase 1919–1939)*. London: The Hogarth Press.

Laub, D., & Lee, S. (2003). Thanatos and massive psychic trauma. *Journal of the American Psychoanalytic Association, 51*:433–463.

Wiener Psychoanalytische Vereinigung (2005). *Trauma der Psychoanalyse?* Vienna: Mille Tre Verlag.

CHAPTER 9

On the history of psychoanalysis in Vienna, with special focus on the forced emigration of psychoanalysts in 1938

Thomas Aichhorn

In this chapter, I would like to provide you with a brief account of a highly significant period in the Vienna Psychoanalytic Society's 100-year history. The Vienna Psychoanalytic Society was founded in 1908 and after 30 years, in 1938, was forced to relinquish its activities due to the takeover by the National Socialists in Austria. Only on April 10, 1946 – now 70 years ago – was it possible to reestablish the Society.

First, I shall be describing the situation in Vienna in the wake of the events in the spring of 1938 as well as some of the aspects responsible for the flight of psychoanalysts from Vienna. Then I shall provide an overview of psychoanalysis in Vienna from 1938 to 1945 and the reopening of the Society in 1946. This overview will be complemented by the two following chapters written by Nadja Pakesch and Tjark Kunstreich. They will give an account of candidates to the Vienna Society whose fates were markedly influenced by the storm of political events that took place in 1938.

During the preparations for this chapter it became clear to me once again that we do not yet possess a comprehensive account of the history of those psychoanalysts who were forced to leave Vienna and their role in the development of psychoanalysis around the world. While there exists an almost incalculable amount of single publications, a complete overview is still missing. In preparation for such a broader exposition, a working group of the Vienna Psychoanalytic Society was formed to go through a list that is kept in the British Psychoanalytic Society's archive. From this list, which shows all members and candidates of the Viennese Society, it is possible to retrieve information about the paths they took during their flight and of the help they received. The biographical sketches presented by Nadja Pakesch and Tjark Kunstreich are the first results of this work.

Vienna during March 1938

Contrary to the widely held opinion that Freud had to be tediously convinced to leave Vienna even as late as March 1938, it should be noted that directly after the invasion of the National Socialists in Austria on Friday, March 11, on the following Sunday, March 13 – the same day the "Anschluss" (annexation) of Austria by Nazi Germany was proclaimed – a board meeting of the Vienna Psychoanalytic Society was held, during which, on Freud's initiative, two decisions were reached: first, that everyone who was able to do so should flee the country, and second, that the Viennese Society was to be relocated to wherever Freud would move. Freud commented: "Following the destruction of the Temple in Jerusalem by Titus, Rabbi Jochanan ben Sakkai asked for permission to build the first Torah-school in Jabne. We are about to do the same thing. Certainly, we have become used to persecution through our history and tradition and some of us have through personal experiences" (Sterba, 1982, p. 164). It was, as Anna Freud had put it in a letter to Jones as early as March 1934 – the time Jewish psychoanalysts fled from Germany – "a new kind of Diaspora" (cf. Steiner, 2000).

Only a few days after said board meeting, on March 16, Anton Sauerwald was appointed by the Austrian National Socialists as acting director of the Vienna Psychoanalytic Society, their outpatient clinic, and the International Psychoanalytical Press. He may have believed that he had been given control of the Society and its institutions and that he would be able to decide their future at his own discretion. In truth, he had no decision-making authority, since both the closure of the association and the publishing house had already been planned and prepared prior to the entry of German troops from Berlin. Not Sauerwald but an SS-Hauptsturmführer from the security forces of the Reichsführer SS, Berlin, was designated to execute the closure. Sauerwald had convened a meeting on March 20, in which the decision was arrived at that a representative of the German Psychoanalytic Society should take over the rights, obligations, and assets of the Vienna Society and publishing house. Ultimately, nothing that had been agreed upon could be implemented, as the representative of the Austrian Chief Medical Officer and one of the security forces of the Reichsführer SS mandated the immediate dissolution of the Society. Its entire property was confiscated and delivered by Sauerwald, who only now was officially authorized to do so, to the "Standstill Commissioner of Clubs, Organizations, and Associations." The outpatient clinic of the Society was taken over by Heinrich Kogerer, and the apartment on the first floor of Berggasse 7, where the Society and the publishing house were accommodated, was seized along with its inventory and taken over by the Oriental Institute of the University of Vienna. The book collections of the publishing house were destroyed (cf. Rothländer, 2008).

The flight of analysts from Vienna

On the same day that memorable board meeting was held, March 13, Anna Freud wrote to Max Eitingon, who had at that time already fled to Jerusalem:

> I just discarded the letter I had begun two days ago; the unfolding events have in the meantime outdated it. I don't want to write too much on the subject, just know that you need not worry and that we are making various plans. As soon as the legal business has been taken care of we will probably travel to Holland. I'll inform you as soon as we know more.
> (Anna Freud, letter to M. Eitingon,
> March 13, 1938; AFP/LoC)

By mid-May of 1938, the Nazis had stepped up the pressure to force the expulsion of Jews from Vienna. The establishment of various bodies, especially those of the "Central Agency for Jewish Emigration in Vienna," was meant to hasten their emigration (Botz, 1980; Rabinovici, 2000). The majority of the Viennese analysts had probably already fled from Vienna between mid-May and mid-July (cf. Reichmayr, 1990, pp. 132ff.).

In 1938, the Viennese Society probably had 68 members (there is no official membership list from 1938) as well as 38 candidates. Not all of them managed to escape in time:

- Rosa Walk was unable to leave Paris, where she had fled to, and probably evaded capture by the Gestapo by committing suicide by jumping from a window.
- Nikola Sugar was deported to Bergen-Belsen and then on to Theresienstadt, where he perished on May 15, 1945.
- Ernst Paul Hoffmann was arrested by the Nazis in Brussels. He was interned in various camps in the South of France, got free in 1942, and went to friends living in Marseille who helped him escape to Switzerland. Finally there, he had to undergo surgery due to a severe stomach disorder and died, weakened by the ordeal of his flight, in December of 1944.
- Robert Hans Jokel fled to France and was interned there. He was the only member of the "old" Society who returned to Vienna in 1946.

But even after escaping successfully and having arrived in relative safety, the Viennese very soon had to face the fact that although they had succeeded in saving their lives, they were now confronted with predominant regional conceptions of psychoanalysis. This meant that they were in danger of losing their ideational home along with the loss of the Viennese Society. In London, to where the Freud family and many others from Vienna had fled, the situation of newcomers was particularly precarious because of the fierce controversies between Vienna and London, which, as is generally known, had already begun before 1938. Without being able to go into detail regarding the Freud/Klein controversy in London – which has been extensively documented in the volume edited by Pearl King and Riccardo Steiner (1991) – I do not want to leave unmentioned how different the living conditions of those participating in the London controversy were. The situation of those who had arrived from Vienna was characterized by politically determined violence and by the collapse of the Viennese Society. Anna Freud's situation, especially, had drastically worsened. As stand-in for her father, leading the Viennese Society together with Paul Federn and since 1935 acting as director of the educational committee, she had over the years become an authority, and even in emigration she was recognized as such by her former Viennese colleagues. She had done work in the deciding bodies of the IPA and she had strengthened her position as a theoretician.

In London, Anna Freud was now confronted with an approach to psychoanalysis that radically contradicted everything that she had considered as the just and commonly advocated "cause" of psycho-analysis. Otto Fenichel had already reported on the conception of psychoanalysis in London in March of 1934 in one of his circular letters: "That the teachings of the English Psychoanalytic Association differ from continental psy[cho]a[nalysis], is a known fact. . . . M[elanie] Klein is regarded as the greatest analyst and the one who completed Freud's work" (1998, p. 49f.). And quoting from the report of an emi-grant from Berlin about the state of psychoanalysis in London: "I would never have become an analyst if I had become acquainted with it here in London, instead I would have regarded it as what it is here, namely a secret science that is being practiced by some very strange people as a hobby" (1998, p. 52).

Given this background, it was not very surprising that Melanie Klein and her following did not welcome the Viennese to the Lon-don Society. But even some of the English psychoanalysts, who were not supporters of Klein, feared that inevitably the conflicts that had hitherto been going on between Vienna and London would now lead to a fierce fight within the British Society itself. It's possible to get an impression of the level of mistrust with which they were taking in the emigrants – despite their great willingness to help people in need – from a letter by James Strachey to Edward Glover. To quote just a few lines from Strachey's letter: "I'm very strongly in favour of compromise at all costs. . . . Why should these wretched fascists and communists invade our peaceful compromising island? – (bloody for-eigners)" (Grosskurth, 1986, p. 257).

The professional existence of many analysts who had managed to escape from Vienna was highly unsafe, not only in London but in the United States as well. On November 21, 1938, Anna Freud wrote from London to Max Eitington:

> The princess [Marie Bonaparte] is going to come by again in 14 days and then we'll hold the first session on the America-question. My own posi-tion on this subject has changed. If this here [in London] is the IPA, then the Americans are right to want to be independent. Seen from Vienna everything seemed to be different.
>
> (Anna Freud, letter to M. Eitingon, November 21, 1938; AFP/LoC)

The American Psychoanalytic Association (APA) denied membership to many respected members of the Viennese Psychoanalytic Society. This was linked to the "America-question" that Anna Freud mentioned in her letter. She was referring to the fiercly-waged conflict between the APA and the IPA over the question of the concession of non-doctors to the training as psychoanalysts and over their membership in different branches of the associations. This issue – Anna Freud and, with her, the Viennese Society were demanding an unrestricted admittance; the APA was opposed to this – almost led to a secession of the APA from the IPA. The APA was finally able to assert itself, and they finally rejected the psychoanalytic training of non-doctors and of the membership of so-called laymen for their region at the IPA congress in the summer of 1938 in Paris. This move also served to crowd out the school of psychoanalytic pedagogy that had been developed largely in Vienna. Otto Fenichel commented on this in his circular letter, dating from June 25, 1938: "Now the Viennese Society is lost and anxiously one asks: What shall become of Psychoanalysis?" (1998, p. 921). And: "Some Years ago a friend asked me . . .: 'Which issues are the primary research topics in Psychoanalysis?' I answered: 'The question whether the Nazis are going to come into power.' – Now they have" (1998, p. 931).

Psychoanalysis in Vienna from 1938 to 1946 (cf. Ash, 2012)

Of the active members of the Vienna Society of 1938, only August Aichhorn, Richard Nepallek, and Alfred Winterstein had remained in Vienna.

Nepallek died in 1940 under mysterious circumstances from a coal-gas poisoning. Winterstein, who had Jewish ancestors, attempted to live life as inconspicuously as possible under the Nazi regime. Aichhorn was the only member of the Viennese Society who became a member of the German Psychoanalytic Society and thus also of the German Institute. An important motive of his course of action was his hope to be able to help his son, who was arrested immediately after the seizure of power by the Nazis and sent to a concentration camp. He was able to continue his private practice more or less unrestricted.

The Nazis had celebrated the closure of the Vienna Society and the destruction of the publishing house as a great success. The *General Journal of Psychiatry* reported: "The stronghold of Jewish Psychotherapy in Vienna has fallen through the Anschluss. It was possible to unite a small group of German psychotherapists in Vienna to form an association. . . . As head of this committee, Prof. Dr. Goering appointed the old party comrade Docent Dr. Kogerer."[1]

Aside from Kogerer, this committee included his affiliate Norbert Thumb, two Adlerians who had remained in Vienna, and the previously mentioned Aichhorn. While Kogerer had taken over the management of the committee, he was to show little interest in it. That is why, as far as we can ascertain today, it never became active.

Independently of this committee, a small working group had formed around Aichhorn in 1938–39. Friedl Aufreiter, one of the participants, described the circumstances of these meetings as follows: "From the winter of 1938–39, weekly conspiratorial meetings were held. We were afraid to be discovered by the Gestapo, so we had no contact with the other participants outside of the seminary in Aichhorn's apartment. Informally, it was strictly analytical training, later, when the seminar was recognized by the German Institute, it was officially therapeutical, in terms of the Institute."[2]

It is not known when and under what circumstances Aichhorn informed Göring of this seminar. In any case, in 1941 the group was officially recognized as a training seminar by the German Institute (cf. Lingens, 1983, p. 145). Participants in the training seminar were those who had already participated in the unofficial training seminars – the couples Aufreiter and Lingens and the members of the Vienna working group of the German Institute – joined in the following years by a few training candidates.

Karl Motesiczky, who had belonged to the first informal group and underwent analysis with Aichhorn, was forbidden to continue to participate in training, however, being a so-called first-degree half breed (cf. Rothländer, 2010). He and Ella and Kurt Lingens were arrested on October 13, 1942, having aided Jews in their escape.[3] Karl Motesiczky died on June 25, 1943, in Block 19, the sick prisoners' barracks of the concentration camp Auschwitz, from typhus (Rothländer, 2003, 2010). Ella Lingens survived her time in the concentration camps Auschwitz and Dachau (Lingens, 1948). Kurt Lingens was transferred to a penal company on the Russian front. He lived to see the liberation of Vienna by the Red Army in a military hospital in Vienna.

Of the training candidates whom Aichhorn supervised during those years, ten became members of the reopened Society in 1946. Igor A. Caruso, who had joined in 1944, founded a new society – independent of the Vienna Psychoanalytic Society – the "Vienna Work Group for Depth Psychology" (today the Vienna Psychoanalytic Association), which was formally constituted in 1947.

It can be deduced from the surviving protocols of the training seminar and Aichhorn's writings to Berlin that he and his students largely adhered to the prescribed language rules. However, within a circle based on trust, because of the familiarity of the members, in training and control analyses the theory of psychoanalysis was probably discussed freely. It was Aichhorn's intention to give young doctors and psychologists as far as it was possible the chance to study genuine psychoanalytic theory and practice even after the official recognition by the German Institute.

The reopening of the society on April 10, 1946
(cf. Aichhorn, 2012)

In the autumn of 1945, Aichhorn received a letter from Anna Freud, dated September 17 of that year. She wrote:

> I was very happy to receive your letter. Thank you very much for writing. It is very good to know that you are all right. . . . Somehow I always felt sure that you would manage to work whatever the outer circumstances were, and that under all conditions people would need you and your help. . . . If you think that it is possible to have an Institute again, then I am sure you are right. Anyway, I would always trust your judgment of any situation.
>
> (Aichhorn, 2012, p. 168)

Anna Freud's letter was obviously a response to a lost letter of Aichhorn asking her consent for reopening the Vienna Society. After the bureaucratic hurdles had been overcome, the dissolution of the Society was rescinded. The formal reopening was set for April 10, 1946. Aichhorn emphasized that the now existing Vienna Psychoanalytic Society should not be considered a new establishment but a continuation of the Society's activities after a forced interruption of eight years.

Many of the Society's former members and some of the European and American institutes sent letters and telegrams of congratulations. Freud's representatives in the leadership of the "old" Vienna Society, Anna Freud and Paul Federn, congratulated as well.

Anna Freud concludes her letter as follows:

> The fact that, during the hard times of national socialism, you managed to continue working on psychoanalysis, to teach and to heal, and in doing so, to carry on the tradition of the institute, fills me with admiration. I wish your new creation the very best in vigour and impact on the surrounding environment. The destruction of psychoanalysis in 1938 was logically inevitable. Psychoanalysis can only prosper where there is freedom of thought. Austria's new-found freedom will, I think, signify a new life for psychoanalytic work.
>
> (Aichhorn, 2012, p. 179f.)

The next step after the reopening of the Society was the request to be recognized again as a branch association of the IPA. Jones confirmed this in the summer of 1946. His decision was unanimously confirmed by the next congress of the IPA, which was held in Zurich in 1949.

As early as in autumn of 1945, Aichhorn had requested help from Anna Freud and Ernst Kris in finding "old" members of the Society willing to come to Vienna to train the new members. He had to wait for an answer to this crucial question for months. A first, dismissive response came from Anna Freud, and Kris also wrote that he could not think of anyone willing to come to Vienna.

In letters that Ruth Eissler, at that time living in Chicago, and Anna Freud exchanged in 1946, one can find what they – for example – thought about Aichhorn's ideas. Ruth Eissler wrote amongst other things: "In the meantime we have been able to establish direct communication with Aichhorn and I am very much impressed by his untiring efforts to preserve Psychoanalysis in Vienna. Of course, we all are very willing to support Aichhorn in his endeavours, but as to his plans to have the former European analysts come to teach in Vienna I feel rather doubtful and personally cannot imagine anyone emotionally ready to do so." And she continues:

> You probably are informed about the situation in Chicago, the prevailing trends in the Chicago Psychoanalytical Society and Institute and the very small opposition group here. . . . If we should be strong enough, at one time not too far away, to establish a second training institute in Chicago, the proposed changes will be a great help; however, if we cannot achieve this goal we certainly will be on the losing end. I think it mainly depends on the willingness for action on the part of those members of the Chicago group who still adhere to the basic principles of psycho-

analysis. So far nothing in the direction I just mentioned has been either formulated or done.

> (R. Eissler, letter to A. Freud, February 2, 1946; original; AFP/LoC)

Anna Freud answered:

A month ago we too were able to communicate directly with Vienna, and Vienna of course means Aichhorn. Before that we had managed to send some letters by way of America, but it is, of course, a very different feeling to be in direct touch. He certainly is an amazing person. He is actually opening the Vienna Institute again and full of enthusiasm and hopes for its future. I do hope that he will find the teachers whom he needs. I did not have the heart to tell him the truth concerning my own attitude towards trips to Vienna whenever that should become possible. He even thought that I might manage to come for the opening of the Institute, which happens, I think, just now. In reality I just cannot imagine ever setting foot into Vienna again for whatever purpose it might be. You see, it is not the distance from Europe that has the effect on people. It is probably something very different that does it. We may all forget what happened in ten or twenty years' time, but at the moment I cannot quite imagine that. . . . I was very interested in everything you wrote about the trends in the Chicago Psychoanalytic Society and Institute. I had known some of the facts before but not all of them. You may be interested to know that I and my friends here are facing a nearly identical situation with regard to the British Society. The main trend here is Melanie Klein's teaching. It is equally difficult to co-operate and to split off. And I do not know what the final outcome will have to be.

> (A. Freud, letter to R. Eissler, March 2, 1946; copy; AFP/LoC)

The majority of members of the re-established Viennese Society consisted of its very first candidates. According to the statutes introduced in 1946, they were obliged to continue the training they had begun under Aichhorn and to complete it in the newly established educational institute of the Society. Otto Fleischmann, who had been in therapy with Aichhorn until the spring of 1939 and went on to become a member and training analyst of the Hungarian Society, and Robert Hans Jokl headed the theoretical training seminars. Jokl also took over the management of the reopened outpatient clinic. The new members of the Society continued their training and control therapy sessions with Aichhorn, Fleischmann, or Jokl.

Aichhorn, who in his particular field of work – the application of psychoanalysis to education and social work – was a thoroughly independent and innovative practitioner and theoretician, distrusted the developments of psychoanalysis in the United States, of which his former students had informed him. In conclusion, to give you an impression of the way Aichhorn imagined the Viennese Society's work, I shall quote a passage from a letter he wrote to a former analysand, Paul Kramer, who was living in Chicago at the time:

> It is with rather great regret that I read in your letter what I have also been reading in Kurt [Eissler's] letters, that psychoanalysis is beginning to move away from Freud. This whole movement seems to me like the pubertal conflicts of adolescent sons, who are unable to deal with their father, and if you'll allow me a critical comment, I would like to say that this movement has to have originated with poorly analyzed people. My function here gets new meaning through your messages: To pre-serve Freudian analysis in the city of its birth, the way it was created by Freud. That does not imply that the 12 Freud volumes should become a single great prayer-book and that we should abandon all research, but our goals and the direction in which we are heading remain clearly established. Maybe decades from now – when I will long have passed on – a time shall come when 'psychotherapists' from all directions, even America, are going to come to Vienna to learn what Freud really taught.
> (August Aichhorn, letter to Paul Kramer,
> September 19, 1946; copy: NAA)

Archives

AFP/LoC = Anna Freud Papers, Archive of the Library of Congress, Washington.
NAA = Estate August Aichhorn, Thomas Aichhorn, Vienna.

Notes

1   Note from the General Magazine for Psychiatry, 1938, 108, p. 410.
2   Interview from May 1997 in London/Canada (Thomas Aichhorn and Friedl Früh).
3   Secret State Police, State Police Chapter Vienna, Daily Report, October 13–15, 1942 (Documentation Centre of Austrian Resistance).

References

Aichhorn, T. (Ed.) (2012). *Anna Freud/August Aichhorn "Die Psychoanalyse kann nur dort gedeihen, wo Freiheit des Gedankens herrscht" Briefwechsel 1921–1949.* Frankfurt am Main: Brandes & Apsel.

Ash, M. (Ed.) (2012). *Materialien zur Geschichte der Psychoanalyse in Wien 1938–1945.* Frankfurt am Main: Brandes & Apsel.

Botz, G. (1980). *Wien vom "Anschluß" zum Krieg. Nationalsozialistische Machtübernahme und politisch-soziale Umgestaltung am Beispiel der Stadt Wien 1938/39.* Vienna: Jugend und Volk.

Fenichel, O. (1998). *119 Rundbriefe.* Frankfurt am Main: Stroemfeld.

Grosskurth, P. (1986). *Melanie Klein.* London: Maresfield.

King, P., & Steiner, R. (Eds.) (1991). *The Freud–Klein Controversies 1941–45.* London: Routledge.

Lingens, E. (1948). *Prisoner of Fear.* London: Victor Gollancz.

Lingens, E. (1983). Psychoanalyse unter dem Nationalsozialistischen Regime. *Sigmund Freud House Bulletin 7*:12–15; In: I. Korotin (Ed.), *"Die Zivilisation ist nur eine ganz dünne Decke . . ." Ella Lingens (1908–2002)* (pp. 143–147). Vienna: Praesens, 2011.

Rabinovici, D. (2000). *Instanzen der Ohnmacht. Wien 1938–1945. Der Weg zum Judenrat. Historische Studie.* Frankfurt am Main: Suhrkamp.

Reichmayr, J. (1990). *Spurensuche in der Geschichte der Psychoanalyse.* Frankfurt am Main: Nexus.

Rothländer, C. (2003). "Wer wird Widerstand leisten, wenn alle gehn . . .". Über Leben und Werk Karl Motesiczkys. *Luzifer-Amor, 16*:39–65.

Rothländer, C. (2008). Zwischen "Arisierung" und Liquidation. Das Schicksal der Wiener Psychoanalytischen Vereinigung nach dem "Anschluss" im März 1938. *Luzifer-Amor, 21*:100–133.

Rothländer, C. (2010). *Karl Motesiczky 1904–1943. Eine biographische Rekonstruktion.* Vienna: Turia + Kant.

Steiner, R. (2000). *It Is a New Kind of Diaspora.* London: Karnac.

Sterba, R. (1982). *Erinnerungen eines Wiener Psychoanalytikers.* Frankfurt am Main: Fischer.

CHAPTER 10

Liselotte Frankl and Hans Herma: two candidates of the Vienna Psychoanalytic Society in 1938

Nadja Pakesch

I have chosen to discuss two candidates of the Vienna Psychoanalytic Society who were forced to leave Austria in 1938. The focus of their biographies lies in their training situation, both in Vienna and in their new destinations, London and New York. I have tried to learn more about their emigration and how they were able to manage building up a new existence in exile.

Liselotte Frankl (1910–1988)

Liselotte Frankl was born on May 18, 1910, in Vienna, the eldest daughter of Julie Baum and the businessman Robert Frankl. After attending a reformed grammar school for girls, she started studying psychology in 1929 at the University of Vienna with Charlotte and Karl Bühler (Weitzel, 2002). Frankl became one of Charlotte Bühler's research assistants (Benetka, 2015). Charlotte Bühler was at the time the only professor of child and developmental psychology in Europe. The two other assistants were Esther Bick and Ilse Hellmann, who also became psychoanalysts after emigrating to England (Steiner, 2000a). In 1934, Frankl's paper *Zum Problem der Funktionsreifung* ("On the Problem of

Maturation of Function") was published together with Lotte Danzinger. The two women analysts tested Albanian children who, following Albanian tradition, had been tied down to their cradles during the first years of their lives.

The Bühlers, who represented a cognitive and observational approach, were strictly opposed to psychoanalysis. But Liselotte Frankl was already interested in psychoanalysis during her university years and secretly attended Anna Freud's lectures at the Vienna Psychoanalytic Training Institute (Yorke, 1989). In fall 1935, Frankl applied as a candidate to the Vienna Psychoanalytic Society. In the records of the training committee meeting of the Vienna Psychoanalytic Society on October 24, 1935, it is stated:

> *Vorsitz: Anna Freud; anwesend: Federn, Aichhorn, Hitschmann, Hartmann, Sterba, Wälder, Grete Bibring; Schriftführer: E. Bibring . . . Frau Dr. Frankl. Dr. phil, Assistentin bei Bühler, wird von Aichhorn u. Frl. Freud sehr empfohlen. Bewirbt sich um eine Gratis-Lehranalyse. Sollte nämlich früher ein Stipendium vom Fond bekommen, inzwischen wurde dieser leider vergeben. – Frl. Freud schlägt ev[entuell] Dr. Kris als Analytiker ausnahmsweise vor, wiewohl er nicht Lehranalytiker ist. Angenommen.*

> [Chair: Anna Freud; present: Federn, Aichhorn, Hitschmann, Hartmann, Sterba, Wälder, Grete Bibring; secretary: E. Bibring. . . . Mrs Frankl, PhD, Bühler's assistant, was strongly recommended by Aichhorn and Miss Freud. She is applying for an analysis fee waiver. Ought to have received a grant from the Fund [set up for this purpose]. Unfortunately, the stipend has already been given to someone else. As an exception, Miss Freud proposes the possibility of Dr Kris as analyst, although he is not a training analyst. Accepted.] (original: Archive Sigmund Freud Museum, London).

Thus, in 1935, Frankl started her training analysis with Ernst Kris. In the same year, she completed her PhD at the University of Vienna. Subsequently, she worked as an educational counsellor at the Youth Welfare Office (Jugendamt) and at the Karolinen Paediatric Hospital in Vienna (Korotin, 2005).

In 1938, after Austria's "Anschluss" to Nazi Germany, Frankl emigrated from Austria to Scotland, Great Britain (Steiner, 2000b). In a list from the Archives of the British Psychoanalytical Society, which mentions all the psychoanalysts who had emigrated from Vienna, Austria, to England and other destinations, the following information about her emigration is recorded:

Is doing analysis with E. Kris. Wishes to come to England to finish her analysis. Will be at least a year before she starts her control analysis. Perhaps has a chance of getting work at the Child Guidance Council, Institute of Medical Psychology (Dr. Calver). You wrote to Frl. Freud that it was a difficult case and that you hoped she was following up her London connections (10.5.38) Heard from the Society for the Protection of Science and Learning that she had been offered a position with Gipsy Hill Training College and Mr. Adams was going to urge for a permit for her. There are also other positions in view for her. (9.6.38) Has arrived in England. ~~c/o Neumark, 6 Belsize Park Gdns., N.W.3~~ .stet. ~~40 York House, Turks Row, S.W.3~~ [crossed out in the original].

In Scotland, Liselotte Frankl worked at the Crichton Royal Hospital in Dumfries and started her medical training at the London School of Medicine for Women and at the University of St. Andrews in Scotland. After her graduation in 1945, she worked as a psychiatrist at the East London Child Guidance Clinic. She continued her psychoanalytic training at the British Psychoanalytical Society (King & Steiner, 1991). Frankl became a member of the British Psychoanalytical Society and was appointed a training analyst a few years later (Yorke, 1989).

In a letter to Ernst Kris dated December 12, 1945, Anna Freud wrote "Frankl: has finished her training and her medical degree and now spends part of a year in Crichton Royal, where Stengel is, to get a grounding in psychiatry. Will surely be very good, and someone to rely on."

On March 21, 1948, Frankl wrote to August Aichhorn about those years:

> *Als ich nach London kam bestand Jones darauf, dass ich Medizin studiere um am englischen psychoanalytischen Institut angenommen zu werden u so studierte ich halt 5 Jahre Medizin u. arbeitete dann 1½ Jahre an einem der besten mental hospitals in Britain . . . Jetzt bin ich aber schon seit 1½ Jahren in London als Psychoanalytiker u arbeite ausserdem an einer Child Guidance Clinic wo fast alle die dort angestellt sind analytisch orientiert sind was die Arbeit sehr interessant macht.*

> [When I came to London, Jones insisted that I should study medicine in order to get accepted at the British Psychoanalytical Institute and that's why I studied medicine for five years and then worked for one and a half years at one of the best mental hospitals in Britain. . . . I have now been a psychoanalyst in London for one and a half years, and I also work at a Child Guidance Clinic. Almost everybody employed there is analytically oriented which makes the work very interesting.]

Liselotte Frankl, who represented the tradition of ego psychology, worked closely with Anna Freud, first at the War Nurseries and later as medical director at the Hampstead Child-Therapy Clinic. She held the latter position for many years. Frankl also worked with Anna Freud on an educational column in the magazine *Nursery World*. In 1948, she replaced Kate Friedlander at the Child Guidance Clinic in Horsham. She became a training analyst and supervisor at the Hampstead program. Together with Ilse Hellmann she carried out a research project on adolescence at the Hampstead Clinic.

In 1961 and 1964, she gave lecturing tours in the United States, including seminars in San Francisco, Denver, and other major American cities. Liselotte Frankl made some important contributions to developmental psychology, general psychiatry, and child psychoanalysis. She wrote on various topics, including how to apply psychoanalytic understanding in child psychotherapy, on problems of diagnosis and interview technique, on the ego's participation in the therapeutic alliance, on problems of adolescence, accident proneness, frustration tolerance, and many others. She retired from her position in 1967. She died in London on October 12, 1988, at the age of 78 (Yorke, 1989).

Hans (John Leonard) Herma (1911–1966)

Hans Herma was born on April 6, 1911, in Vienna. His Protestant father came from a family of weavers from Silesia and his Catholic mother from a Slovenian family of winemakers.

After receiving a pedagogy degree, he began his studies in German philology at the University of Vienna, only to switch to psychology soon thereafter. He studied with Charlotte and Karl Bühler. In 1935, he worked as a librarian at the Institute of Psychology at the University of Vienna (Herma, 1936a). In June 1936, he applied as a candidate to the Vienna Psychoanalytic Society. In a letter to Edward Bibring, dated July 6, 1936, Herma wrote that he was accepted. (Herma, 1936a, 1936b) He started his training analysis with Berta Bornstein shortly thereafter (Ginzberg & Bergmann, 1966). In 1937, Herma was employed at the Institute of Psychology, which entertained a difficult relationship to psychoanalysis (Benetka, 1995). This is addressed in the following letter written by Hans Herma to Anna Freud dated January 15, 1937:

Frau Bornstein hatte die Liebenswürdigkeit, meine Teilnahme an dem Dienstag-Kurs von Fenichel und dem Traumkolloquium von Kris zu befürworten und mich anzumelden. Inzwischen hat sich meine äußere Situation am Psychologischen Institut, an dem ich angestellt bin, etwas verändert (ich werde wieder von den Professoren Bühler als Nachfolger des scheidenden Hauptassistenten Dr. Brunswik in Betracht gezogen). Es ist wahrscheinlich, daß man an eine Ernennung die Bedingung knüpft, daß ich nicht an den offiziellen Ausbildungskursen teilnehme, während die Lehranalyse und das Medizinstudium schon jetzt als meine Privatsache erklärt wurde. Falls es dazu kommt, daß ich diese Stelle bekomme, müßte ich die notwendigen Kurse als private nehmen, was mir bei der Verbesserung meiner materiellen Situation möglich wäre.

[Mrs Bornstein kindly supported my participation at Fenichel's Tuesday lectures and Kris' dream colloquium and has enrolled me. Meanwhile the situation at the Institute of Psychology, where I work, has changed a little bit (I am again being considered by Professors Bühler as a potential successor to the outgoing Main Assistant Dr Brunswik). My nomination may be tied to the condition that I do not enrol in official training courses. The training analysis and my studies in medicine have already been declared as my private affair. If I get this position, I will be attending the necessary courses as a private person, which should be possible due to my improved financial situation.]

(Benetka, 1995, pp. 248–249)

In 1938, Herma received his PhD at the Institute of Psychology at the University of Vienna (Geuter, 1986, p. 266). In the Archives of the British Psychoanalytical Society there is an entry about Herma's plans to emigrate: "Vienna, 16. Speckbachergasse 6/26. Doctor's degree of Philosophy. Wishes to continue study of medicine. Send all papers to Dr. Kubie." The same year, Herma emigrated to Switzerland where he joined the research group of Jean Piaget at the Rousseau Institute in Geneva (Ginzberg & Bergmann, 1966). In 1938, he wrote to the Emergency Committee of the American Psychoanalytical Association about working opportunities in the United States and the possibility of securing an affidavit. The committee secured an affidavit for him, intervened with the State Department on his behalf, and renewed his affidavit. The journey, amounting to $214, which he was not asked to repay, was paid by the committee (Warburg, 1948, p. 15).

In 1940, he arrived in the United States. Ernst Kris and Lawrence Kubie supported Herma's emigration (Ginzberg & Bergmann, 1966).

With help from the American Committee for Christian German Refugees, Herma applied for a limited one-year employment at the St. Lawrence University in September 1940. He asked the Emergency Committee in Aid of Displaced Foreign Scholars (http://displaced-scholars.wordpress.com) for the modest support of $450. His Viennese professor Karl Bühler sent a cable of recommendation. The approval committee rejected his application for the grant on the grounds that Herma was considered too young of age (he was only 29 at the time) and the fact that the position could also be filled by an American citizen. He submitted an application again, this time requesting only half the amount of what he had asked for before. His application was this time approved (Fleck, 2015, p. 234).

Herma moved to Canton, New York, and became a lecturer at a small college, St. Lawrence University, also in Canton. After six months teaching there, he was seen again by the Emergency Committee of the American Psychoanalytical Association, where he was recommended to look for a stenographic job while completing his analysis (Warburg, 1948, p. 15). During this time, Hans Herma tried to translate two books by Piaget, but this project failed (Fleck, 2015, p. 235).

In 1941, Hans Herma changed his name to John L. Herma and moved to Manhattan, New York. (www.fdrlibrary.marist.edu/) From 1941 to 1943, he became a research assistant at the Totalitarian Communication project, working with Ernst Kris and Hans Speier at the New School for Social Research in New York. In February 1942, Herma held two lectures jointly with Ernst Kris at the New School For Social Research (Fleck, 2015, p. 235): the first was on Freud's Concept of Phylogenetic Development, the second on Recent Psychoanalytic Theories on the Development of the Child.

Herma joined the US Army and became a US citizen early. During the war, from 1943 to 1945, he worked at the Office of Strategic Service and at the Office of War Information. Herma was a collaborator on the project German Radio Propaganda run by Ernst Kris and Hans Speier at the New School for Social Research (Fleck, 2015, p. 235).

From 1945 to 1950, he was assistant professor at New York University. John Herma collaborated with Eli Ginzberg, a professor of economics at Columbia University in New York. He applied a developmental approach to their study and publication *Occupational Choice*, a theory of career choice, and helped establish a theoretical foundation in the field of counselling and guidance. Anna Freud considered this book a major contribution to ego psychology (Ginzberg & Bergmann, 1966).

Herma held a private practice for psychotherapy since 1946. Herma held the position of a faculty member in various psychoanalytical training institutions and at the National Psychological Association for Psychoanalysis for 14 years. Hans (John L.) Herma died in New York on September 20, 1966 (Ginzberg & Bergmann, 1966; Geuter, 1986, p. 266).

References

Works on Liselotte Frankl

Benetka, G. (2015). Frankl, Liselotte. In: U. Wolfradt, E. Billmann-Mahecha & A. Stock (Eds.), *Deutschsprachige Psychologinnen und Psychologen 1933– 1945. Ein Personenlexikon* (pp. 123–124). Berlin: Springer.

Frankl, L. (1948). Unpublished letter to August Aichhorn. Estate of August Aichhorn. Thomas Aichhorn, Vienna.

Freud, A. (1945). Unpublished letter to Ernst Kris. Collections of the Manuscript Division, Library of Congress, Washington, DC.

King, P., & Steiner, R. (1991). *The Freud-Klein Controversies 1941–45*. London: Routledge.

Korotin, I. (2005). Frankl, Liselotte. Wissenschaftlerinnen und Remigration – Die "Austrian University League of America". *IWK-Mitteilungen*, 1–2:9.

Steiner, R. (2000a). *Tradition, Change, Creativity: Repercussions of the New Diaspora on Aspects of British Psychoanalysis*. London: Karnac.

Steiner, R. (2000b). *"It Is a New Kind of Diaspora", Explorations in the Socio-politcal and Cultural Context of Psychoanalysis*. London: Karnac.

Weitzel, U. (2002). Frankl, Liselotte. In: B. Keintzel & I. Korotin (Eds.), *Wissenschaftlerinnen in und aus Österreich. Leben – Werk – Wirken* (p. 184). Vienna: Böhlau.

Yorke, C. (1989). Liselotte Frankl: An Obituary. *Bulletin of the Anna Freud Centre*, 12:85–86. www.psychoanalytikerinnen.de [last accessed 1 September 2017].

Works (selection) by Liselotte Frankl

Frankl, L. (1935). *Lohn und Strafe. Ihre Bedeutung in der Familienerziehung.* Jena: Fischer.

Frankl, L. (1961). Some observations on the development and disturbances of integration in childhood. *Psychoanalytical Study Child,* 16:146–163.

Frankl, L. (1963a). Self-preservation and accident proneness in children and adolescents. *Psychoanalytical Study Child,* 18:464–483.

Frankl, L. (1963b). A specific problem in adolescent boys: Difficulties in loosening the infantile tie to the mother. *The Bulletin of the Philadelphia Association for Psychoanalysis,* 13(3):120–129.

Frankl, L. (1964). Die Hampstead Child Therapy Clinic. In: P. Federn & H. Meng (Eds.), *Psychoanalyse und Alltag.* Bern: Huber.

Frankl, L. (1965). Susceptibility to accidents: A developmental study. *British Journal of Medical Psychology,* 38:289–297.

Frankl, L., & Danzinger, L. (1934). Zum Problem der Funktionsreifung. Erster Bericht über Entwicklungsprüfungen an albanischen Kindern. *Zeitschrift für Kinderforschung,* 43:219–254.

Frankl, L., & Hellman, I. (1962). The ego's participation in the therapeutic alliance. *International Journal of Psychoanalysis,* 43:333–334.

Works on Hans Herma

Benetka, G. (1995). *Psychologie in Wien: Sozial- und Theoriegeschichte des Wiener Psychologischen Instituts 1922–1938.* Vienna: WUV-Universitätsverlag.

Emergency Committee EC. File Herma, John Leonard. Box 14, New York Public Library, New York.

Fleck, C. (2015). *Etablierung in der Fremde. Vertriebene Wissenschaftler in den USA nach 1933.* Frankfurt am Main: Campus Verlag.

Geuter, U. (1986). *Daten zur Geschichte der deutschen Psychologie: Psychologische Institute, Fachgesellschaften, Fachzeitschriften, Biographien, Emigranten 1879–1945 (Band 1).* Göttingen: Hogrefe.

Ginzberg, E., & Bergmann, M. (1966). John L. Herma: In memoriam: Two addresses. *The Psychoanalytical Review,* 53D:173–177.

Herma, H. (1936a). Unpublished Curriculum Vitae, 15 June 1936. Archive Sigmund Freud Museum, London.

Herma, H. (1936b). Unpublished letter to Edward Bibring. Archive Sigmund Freud Museum, London.

http://displacedscholars.wordpress.com/ ("103.) Herma, John Leonard") [last accessed 1 September 2017].

Warburg, B. (1948). Summary of the work of the Emergency Committee on Relief and Immigration of the American Psychoanalytic Association, 1938–1948. Archives, American Psychoanalytic Association, Oskar Diethelm Library, Weill Cornell Medical College.

www.fdrlibrary.marist.edu/_resources/images/wrb/wrb0448.pdf ("List of our refugee scholars", Folder 39, New School of Social Research, 19 April 1944) [last accessed 1 September 2017].

Works (selection) by Hans Herma

Herma, H. (1938). *Die Bildhaftigkeit des Films*. Vienna.

Herma, H., Kris, E., Speier, H., Axelrad, S., & Loeb, J. (Eds.) (1944). *German Radio Propaganda: Report on Home Broadcasts During the War*. London: Oxford University Press.

Herma, H., & Kurth, G. M. (Eds.) (1950). *Elements of Psychoanalysis*. Cleveland: World Publishing.

Herma, J. L., & Ginzberg, E. (1964). *Talent and Performance*. New York: Columbia University Press.

Herma, J. L., Ginzberg, E., Anderson, J. K., & Ginsburg, S. W. (Eds.) (1959). *The Ineffective Soldier: Lessons for Management and the Nation. The Lost Divisions (Volume 1), Breakdown and Recovery (Volume 2), Patterns of Performance (Volume 3)*. New York: Columbia University Press.

Herma, J. L., Ginzberg, E., Berg, I. E., & Brown, C. A. (Eds.) (1966). *Lifestyles of Educated Women*. New York: Columbia University Press.

Herma, J. L., Ginzberg, E., Ginsburg, S. W., & Axelrad, S. (Eds.) (1951). *Occupational Choice: An Approach to a General Theory Book*. New York: Columbia University Press.

CHAPTER 11

Remembering Dr Otto Brief

Tjark Kunstreich

We know about those candidates of the Vienna Psychoanalytic Society who survived World War II and the Holocaust only because they survived. This simple but drastic fact allows us to trace their lives even when they did not continue to work as psychoanalysts. We know much less about those who perished in concentration camps. Indeed, till this day, we still do not know the exact number of candidates and affiliated educators of the Vienna Psychoanalytic Society. It is unlikely that we ever will know about all of them. Here I will discuss the fate of one of those candidates, Otto Brief, thereby hoping to a pay a small tribute to all those other candidates who died, as well as to all those who tried to save them.

My research sheds a light on the fate of Jewish psychoanalysts in Eastern Europe, of whom we know almost nothing. Otto Brief was a member of the psychoanalytic Study Group in Prague, which was part of the Vienna Society. The Study Group was founded in 1933 by Czechoslovakian sympathizers of psychoanalysis and German emigrants, such as Frances Deri and Otto Fenichel, who left Berlin for Prague in the hope that the Nazi regime would not last, an illusion shared by many of their left-wing contemporaries. Frances Deri arrived in Prague in 1933; Fenichel emigrated first to Oslo, arriving in Prague only in 1935. Annie

Reich joined Deri in Prague in 1933. Until Fenichel's arrival, Reich and Stefi Bornstein were the only two training analysts in Prague.

Otto Brief was born in Vronov on December 31, 1891. At the time of his birth the small village was called Frain an der Thaya and was part of the Austro-Hungarian Empire. Brief studied medicine and was one of the founding members of the Prague Study Group. His wife Marie, a kindergarten educator born in 1906, was also a member of the Study Group. The family had two children: Vera was born in 1928, Felix in 1929. The family lived in Olmutz, today Olomouc in the Czech Republic, No. 1, Palacky-Str., in a bourgeois apartment house in the inner city.

On January 29, 1940, the New York psychoanalyst Bettina Warburg, the secretary of the Emergency Committee on Relief and Immigration (ECRI) of the American Psychoanalytic Association, wrote to the Norwegian psychoanalyst Harald Schjelderup and asked for his support with regard to Marie Brief, who at the time was still living with her children in Olmutz. In this letter, Warburg wrote that the Emergency Committee had unsuccessfully tried to obtain the release of Dr Brief from the concentration camp and to arrange for his emigration. Apparently, Otto Brief was at the time imprisoned in a concentration camp near Berlin. Warburg writes:

> There was at first some doubt about whether Dr Brief was still alive, as his clothes were returned to his wife, and the information that he had been transferred to the concentration camp at Oranienburg was given out subsequently. I do not need to amplify for you what the incarceration in this particular camp means, particularly as the German authorities have stated that there is no question of releasing Dr Brief before the termination of the war. Mrs Brief has been notified that she must leave Olmutz before March 1, together with her two children. This is a particularly distressing situation for her, and from the information we are able to obtain, she is anxious to remain in Europe.
>
> (Original letter)

Warburg asked Schjelderup whether it would be possible to arrange documents for Marie Brief and her children so that they could emigrate to Norway for a short time. Marie Brief had been recommended to also write to the psychoanalyst Stefi Pedersen, but Warburg did not have Pederson's address. Warburg informed Schjelderup that there was funding in the United States to help the family to emigrate to South America, but that this money could also be used for the emigration to

Norway. This important letter was discovered by Nellie Thompson, the archivist of the New York Psychoanalytic Society and Institute in the papers of Annie Reich, to whom Warburg had sent a copy.

In the minutes of the meeting of the American Psycho-Analytic Association (APSaA) in May 1940, the Emergency Committee reported on the Briefs:

> Unfortunately your Committee was unable to be of any real assistance to Dr. and Mrs. Otto Brief, since the German government retracted its initial promise to release Dr. Brief from prison upon the completion of emigration arrangements, and instead transferred him to Oranienburg. Mrs. Brief appealed for help so that she and her children might go to Norway. Dr. Hanns Sachs and Dr. Max Eitingon generously supplied the necessary funds; but these arrangements could not be completed because hostilities broke out in Norway.

On April 9, 1940, Nazi Germany had occupied Norway.

In the Yad Vashem database we find the following information: Otto Brief was arrested on May 26, 1939, in Prague. Two months before, the Wehrmacht had occupied the last parts of the Czech Republic after the annexation of the Sudetenland in fall 1938. Some sources state that Brief had tried to flee together with his colleague Therese Bondy. She, too, was a member of the Prague Study Group and was later murdered in Auschwitz, together with her husband Hugo and their son.

Initially, Otto Brief was a political prisoner. The German files read: "Reason of arrest: Communist attitude; protective custody ordered by the Staatspolizei Prague on May 26, 1939." Protective custody – in German *Schutzhaft* – meant imprisonment without trial. On December 4, 1939, Brief was transferred to the Bavarian prison of Hof, where he received the number 2423. The file now reads: "protective custody, political, Jew." Only three days later, Brief was deported to the Sachsenhausen concentration camp, which was at that time the largest Nazi camp. In Sachsenhausen, Brief received the prisoner number 14892/10151; again, ten months later, on September 5, 1940, he was transferred to the Dachau concentration camp near Munich, where he received the prisoner number 17847; on July 12, 1941, Brief was sent to the Buchenwald camp, prisoner number 8680, and finally he was transferred to Auschwitz on October 19, 1941, where he was assigned the number 68378. Otto Brief died in Auschwitz in December 1942. The cause of his death is unknown.

Marie Brief and her children left Olmutz before March 1, 1940, probably for Prague. They were deported from Prague to the Theresienstadt Ghetto on September 4, 1942, with the transport "Bd." On October 6, 1944, they were transferred with the transport "Eo" to Auschwitz and were immediately sent to the gas chambers. In this train there were 1550 people; only 112 survived. From Olmutz, 3489 Jews were deported; only 285 survived. There was no Jewish community in Olmutz as recently as 1991.

The summary of the Emergency Committee, written in 1948, notes Dr Otto Brief as "deceased": "German Psychoanalyst. Interned in a German concentration camp, where he died. Mrs. Brief and their two children were trying to get to Norway from Germany. The Emergency Committee paid $ 1,740.00 for their transportation to the United States but they were unable to leave because of the war. The money was refunded later."

Ernst Federn, the psychoanalyst and social worker who was imprisoned in Buchenwald, reported that he had met Otto Brief in Buchenwald, and that he had supervised Federn's observations of their fellow inmates. Federn described Brief as a follower of Wilhelm Reich, who had been Brief's analyst. Federn also said that Brief had perished in Auschwitz. The possibility that Brief may indeed have been a follower of Wilhelm Reich is further corroborated by the plan to emigrate to Norway and Marie Brief's personal contact to Stefi Pedersen, who started her training with the Berlin Institute in 1930 and left Germany for Norway with her training analyst Otto Fenichel in 1933. These are the very few traces I have found. Until now, it was assumed that Brief died in 1943 in Buchenwald or Dachau.

The sum of over $1700 that was provided by the Emergency Committee to support the emigration of Marie Brief and her children was generous in comparison to other cases, typically supported with sums between $40 and $300. Today $1700 would be equivalent to over $33,000. This suggests that there was a realistic sense within the psychoanalytic community of the immediate threat to its members and at the same time a commitment to helping them escape. This contradicts the often repeated allegations of ignorance amongst psychoanalysts.

Otto Brief's frequent transfers within the concentration camp system, as well as the measures against his family, suggest he may have been an important prisoner because of his medical training.

It is not known whether Hans Sachs and Max Eitingon, both eminent members of the Berlin Institute and the German Psychoanalytic Society, knew Otto Brief personally. The reference to Brief in some documents as a "German analyst" could indicate he received part of his training in Berlin prior to moving to Prague.

The example of Otto Brief and his family shows that there is still a lot about the biographies of psychoanalysts and candidates during the Nazi domination of Europe that we do not know. This chapter is far from being closed.

INDEX

addiction to near-death *see* Joseph,
  Betty
Adler, Alfred 122
Adorno, Theodor W. 128
Aichhorn, August 140, 156–159
Aichhorn, Thomas 18, 142
American Psychoanalytic Association
  (APsaA) 156, 158, 167, 174, 175
Analysis Terminable and Interminable
  56, 62
Antigone 130–132
Anschluss 137–138; impact on the
  Vienna Group 139–142, 152–156,
  164
Aufreiter, Friedl 157
auto-eroticism 57

Beland, Hermann 79–80
Bell, David 37
"Beyond the Pleasure Principle" 1, 2,
  4–7, 17; Laplanche's reading of *see*
  Laplanche, Jean; introduction of
  death drive in 2, 61
Birksted-Breen, Dana 77–78
Brief, Otto 173
British Psychoanalytic Society 8

Britton, Ronald 108
Butler, Judith 113

castration (symbolic) 129, 131, 133
"Civilization and Its Discontents" 8,
  18, 109; life-death drive concepts
  in 71; on the renunciation of drives
  123; and the Vienna Group 142–
  145; *see also* malaise
"Child Is Being Beaten, A" 45–49
creationism 124; *see also* Darwin,
  Charles

Darwin, Charles 124; *see also* theory
  of evolution
death: denial of 122; fear of 9, 30, 37,
  51, 63, 79, 83, 108; and immortality
  133; and the symbolic order 129, 133
death drive: British and American
  perspectives on 8–11; as
  "creationist sublimation" 131;
  current views of 14–16; debates
  over 2; denial of concept of 40, 116;
  as desire of death 131, 133; dualism
  of 126; French perspectives on
  11–13; key premises of 28; Kleinian